Praise for *Sale*

"April Dunford has done it again! She's b̶e̶e̶n̶ ̶k̶n̶o̶w̶n̶ as the GOAT of positioning ... and she's now tackling sales with brio! *Sales Pitch* is chock-full of practical, real-world advice on how to use a story to sell. A must-read for teams who want to scale and outperform!"

BRUNO AZIZA, head of data and analytics at Google Cloud

"Working with April Dunford taught our company why positioning is important and how to actually do it. April's workshop taught us why customers can be oblivious to the qualities of your product if you don't speak the right language. I have gifted and recommended *Obviously Awesome* to many people, and I will be doing the same for *Sales Pitch!*"

ABHINAV ASTHANA, co-founder and CEO of Postman

"April Dunford is the best of what is out there—and adding her special sauce. If you're going to read a sales book, read this one. And if you're going to read a strategy book, read this one. I recommend this book for leaders across the organization, including the C-suite. Like April's broader positioning work, *Sales Pitch* is about more than sales or marketing. It gets to the heart of a company's strategy and the various interdependencies that need to be in place for great positioning and then sales to work."

LINDSEY PADRINO, SVP of strategy and business operations at Skillsoft

"April Dunford is a genius at providing founders with tools to connect with customers through product positioning. *Sales Pitch* is a must-read book to help scale your sales and marketing."

ANNA SAINSBURY, co-founder and CEO of GeoComply

"In *Obviously Awesome*, April Dunford offered a new way to think about positioning and the tools to do it yourself. In *Sales Pitch*, she has done it again—this time challenging how you think about pitching and making sure you're equipped to create your own compelling product proposition."

PAUL DOYLE, head of corporate strategy at Epic Games

"April Dunford's approach works! This book is a must-read for any founder."

NICK FRANCIS, co-founder and CEO of Help Scout

"As a CEO, one of your most important jobs is to help articulate your company's point of view into a compelling sales presentation that tells your story and positions your product as the obvious choice. We went on this journey with April Dunford and it was transformational for our business. *Sales Pitch* is the book to read if you are a founder, CEO, or marketing or sales professional of a B2B technology company looking to win in your market."

FREDRIK SKANTZE, co-founder and CEO of Funnel

"If you're a B2B marketer and you haven't read April Dunford's books, where have you been? After her *Obviously Awesome* tour de force, April goes straight to where positioning gets really real: the sales pitch. With clear explanations and a dash of wit, April teaches us not only how to structure a winning pitch, but also how to drive alignment within our organization as the pitch is built. *Sales Pitch* is a high-ROI buy."

BRYAN SISE, VP of product and customer marketing at Checkr

SALES
P!TCH

How to Craft a Story to Stand Out and Win

APRIL DUNFORD

BESTSELLING AUTHOR OF **OBVIOUSLY AWESOME**

SALES

P!TCH

Ambient Press

ISBN 978-1-9990230-2-7 (paperback)
ISBN 978-1-9990230-3-4 (ebook)

Published by Ambient Press
aprildunford.com/books

Produced by Page Two
pagetwo.com

Edited by Sarah Brohman
Copyedited by Steph VanderMeulen
Proofread by Alison Strobel
Cover, interior design, and
illustrations by Taysia Louie

aprildunford.com

*To Eric Dunford—a great salesperson
and a heck of a storyteller*

CONTENTS

INTRODUCTION

. . . .

THE WORLD IS FULL OF GREAT BOOKS ABOUT SELLING. But
there's one aspect of selling that doesn't get much attention
from the experts—the sales pitch. I've read books on how to
get meetings, how to handle objections, how to do qualification, and how to negotiate, all of which are unquestionably
important sales skills. This book is about how to build a great
sales pitch. But I warn you, it's not about selling. This is a book
about helping customers buy.

More than a simple product walkthrough, more than a
canned set of discovery questions, more than a pushy sales
monologue, this book gives you a blueprint for building a pitch
that helps your team form a respectful relationship with buyers, clearly position your product's unique strengths, and teach
your prospects what they need to know to confidently move
forward with a purchase decision. But before I get into all that,
let me tell you why I think a book about building a great sales
pitch is needed now more than ever.

Rocket Science?

I started my career as a product marketing manager at a start-up that sold complicated database software to technical buyers. A key part of my job was to work with the sales team to build the slides and the demonstration we used in initial meetings with prospects. We didn't have a structure for this pitch. We pulled together pieces we had seen in other pitches: an "about us" slide, a slide with a bunch of customer logos, a set of slides explaining the product's main features that fit together with a product walkthrough demo showing the breadth of what it could do. The pitch didn't need to be rocket science, did it?

As I progressed in my career, I became a marketing executive and an expert in positioning. Positioning defines how your product is the best in the world at delivering something a certain type of customer really cares about. Positioning is the answer to the question, "Why pick us over the alternatives?"

Unfortunately, it became clear to me that most efforts at product positioning were dying the minute a customer walked into their first call with a sales rep. The marketing team, which was working in a silo, wasn't arming the sales team with a story that helped them strongly position the product against those of their competitors. Sales reps, though skilled at understanding customers, engaging, and negotiating, were losing deals because customers couldn't figure out what made the products different and special versus everything else out there. Our pitches were lifeless product walkthroughs, drowning customers in a river of features that looked and sounded like every other product on the market.

The Power of Positioning

Great positioning is worthless if it can't be turned into a pitch that the sales team can use to close business. It isn't enough to have strong product positioning that gets used only by the marketing department. That positioning needs to be communicated with a story that everyone on the sales team can use.

Positioning has now been my passion for over thirty years: first in my twenty-five-year career as an executive responsible for running marketing, sales, and product teams at a series of seven venture-backed start-ups, and then for another decade as a consultant working with fast-growing technology companies ranging from breakout Series A start-ups to global giants like Google and Epic Games. My job is to help tech companies make it completely clear to customers why their product is different and better than the alternatives in the market.

In 2019, I wrote *Obviously Awesome*, a book about positioning based on my experience working on positioning for over two hundred tech companies. In that book, I describe the methodology I have developed and honed over the past decades to help technology companies ensure their products stand out and win business even in an extremely crowded market. This method helps you do two things. First, it helps you precisely define the value your product delivers that no alternative in the market can. And second, it teaches you how to position that to customers in a way that makes the product ... obviously awesome.

What You'll Learn in This Book

This book is going to teach you how to take your positioning and turn it into a sales pitch that helps your customers understand exactly how your product is different and better than everything else on the market. I'm going to give you a simple, step-by-step process to build a pitch that even an inexperienced salesperson can use to successfully communicate your differentiated value and win business. I've tested and fine-tuned this process over the past fifteen years working on over two hundred sales pitches. I've used this method with very early-stage companies where the only salesperson was the founder and I've used it with large corporations with hundreds of sales reps. It has worked for them, and I believe it will work for you.

Sales Pitch gives you a framework for building a sales narrative that will change your relationship with new prospects and how they perceive your products. You will learn how to win better customers—and more of them.

PART
ONE

DO YOU SELL OR DO YOU HELP CUSTOMERS BUY?

· ·

I work with the founders and CEOs of technology companies, many of whom have a background in engineering and tech. The most common complaint I get from these people is that "selling is hard!"

For those of us who started on the technology side of the house, tech is our comfort zone. But most tech leaders quickly learn that for the company and its products to survive, they have to get good at sales. At the end of the day, there is no such thing as a "great" product that nobody uses.

Buying Is Hard

I'd like you to think about what it's like to be a buyer for a minute. You might think selling is hard, but I'm going to make the argument that buying is even harder. Now, I know what you're thinking: "Are you kidding me, April? Buying isn't hard, it's easy! It's fun, even! I wish I could just spend my entire day buying stuff!" But I know what you're imagining when you say that. You're picturing yourself buying a nice pair of shoes, or a good meal, maybe a new cellphone. But what if you were shopping for life insurance? How about buying a house? Not so fun anymore, is it? That's because not all purchases are the same. And some purchases are more difficult than others.

Considered and Unconsidered Purchases

In marketing, we make a distinction between "considered" and "unconsidered" purchases. Typically, an unconsidered purchase is easier to make than a considered purchase.

An unconsidered purchase is something you buy without much planning or forethought. This includes everyday consumer products like toothpaste, a sandwich for lunch, or a pack of gum. You don't do much, if any, research ahead of time. Yes, you might compare your options, but mainly you limit your choices to whatever is in front of you at that moment. The stakes for an unconsidered purchase are low. If you make a poor choice you're unhappy with later, it's not a big deal—you will just be sure not to buy it again.

Considered purchases take more time and effort because there are potentially negative consequences if you make a poor choice. Buying a house or purchasing life insurance are examples of considered purchases where the impact of making a bad choice is high. A poor decision could cost you and your family an incredible amount of money. There are many options to choose from and buyers will spend some time educating themselves on what choices are available. In a considered purchase, there are often other people impacted by the decision who might be involved in the purchase process, making it even harder and more time-consuming to make a final decision.

Most technology purchased by businesses, from accounting software to project management tools, are highly considered purchases. The stakes are high in a business purchase. Often, the purchase must be justified to a manager who might question your competence if you make a bad recommendation. Users might be upset if your newly selected product is difficult to use. Bad technology could impact the performance of the business and, in extreme cases, cost the purchaser their job. In short, buying software for a business is nothing like buying a new pair of shoes.

We dramatically underestimate how difficult it is to make a considered purchase decision. As sellers, we are often so preoccupied with how difficult it is to sell a product that we completely lose sight of how buyers are feeling during the purchase process. We are so close to our own offerings that we assume they are easy to understand and to decide to purchase, but frequently this is not the case. Before I give you a business-to-business (B2B) technology example, let me give you a non-technology example of a purchase process that I assumed would be easy and turned out to be frustratingly difficult.

April Buys a Toilet

I live in Toronto, a great city filled with old houses. I recently bought one of these old houses, and in it was an old bathroom. After I hired a contractor to renovate the bathroom, he told me to go choose a new toilet. I had never bought a toilet before, but I thought to myself, "No problem, I'll just run over to the toilet store and pick one out."

In the toilet store, I was immediately approached by a salesperson who asked if they could help me. I said, "Yes, I'm here to buy a toilet." His immediate response was, "Great! What kind of toilet are you looking for?"

Up until this exact moment, I hadn't thought about my toilet requirements beyond, you know, flushing. So, I said,

"Customers, it turns out, are much less worried about missing out than they are about messing up."

MATTHEW DIXON & TED MCKENNA

"I don't really know what kind of toilet I need." He looked slightly disappointed and directed me to the back of the store. "Go have a look," he said. "All of the toilets are there, and the prices and features are listed for each one. Find what you want and let me know, and I will get it for you."

I went to the back, and I saw what seemed like thousands of toilets. Every toilet looked the same and yet they were not the same. Some cost hundreds of dollars, a few cost thousands. They each had a bewildering number of technical features, like gravity assist, siphon flush, and a variety of trapways and tank fittings. There is something called a flapper—some have it, some don't, and I have no idea what a flapper is. I came to the sudden realization that I didn't know how to buy a toilet.

I went home and did some toilet research. I discovered that toilets have a lot of features, apparently thousands of them, and each of those features made little sense to me. I looked at review sites and comparison sites that seemed to narrow down the choices to dozens of recommended toilets, but there were still way too many to choose from. I learned things about toilets I wish I didn't know (did you know there is something called a MaP score that measures the amount of solid waste a toilet can handle in a single flush? There are toilets out there that could flush a small dog, if necessary).

At this point, I was officially frustrated. I'm a busy person with a demanding job and kids and a small dog who doesn't need to be flushed. I didn't have time to become a toilet expert, but I also sure as heck didn't want to pick a bad toilet that left me calling a plumber every week.

And then I got a genius idea: Maybe I didn't have to buy a new toilet. Maybe I could just stick with the old one. Sure, it wasn't new, but it seemed to be working just fine, and, hey, if it started to give me problems down the road, I could deal with it then, when I wasn't in the middle of a bathroom construction project. I had invested three weeks of my time visiting toilet showrooms and researching toilet features, and how many toilets had I purchased? Zero.

How Hard Is It to Buy Your Stuff?

Think about this for a minute. If it's this hard to buy a toilet, how hard is it to buy your product? We all know what a toilet is. We are all long-time toilet users. Your product, however, might be something that folks have never seen or used before. Your product features—with advanced analytics, machine learning, automation, and who knows what else—are likely much more complicated than flappers and trapways. You might be operating in a market where there are dozens of credible alternatives, and you are selling to customers who are using a status quo solution that really is good enough. I can almost guarantee it's much harder for prospects to buy your stuff than it is for me to purchase a toilet.

Solving the "How to Buy" Problem

As it turns out, that was not the end of my toilet story. When I told my contractor my decision to stick with the old toilet, he explained that he had already recycled it and, by the way, he would need the new toilet by the end of the week. I've never been so disappointed in my life.

I went back to the toilet store. A new salesperson asked if he could help me, and I said, "I have a toilet emergency!" He replied, "Hey, I get it. With so many options, it's really hard to choose a toilet, but don't worry, I'm going to teach you how to buy one."

"Teach me, toilet Obi-Wan," I said. "Because I have no idea what I'm doing, but I can't leave here without a toilet."

"There are only three things you need to worry about with toilets," my guide explained. "Quality, aesthetics, and space. Most of the technical features you've been seeing in toilets are all about improving the number of flushes a toilet can handle before it breaks. The more expensive ones last longer than the lower-quality, cheaper ones. You might think you should always go for higher quality, but that's not always the case. If it isn't your primary toilet—for example, if it's going to be in the basement or for a seasonal property—you're fine to go with one of the cheaper toilets because it's rarely going to get flushed."

I told him this was for my primary bathroom, and that instantly eliminated half of the toilets. A good start!

He then moved on to aesthetics. "Some folks want a certain look in their bathroom. Some folks want a gold toilet or a very modern toilet. If you want that, you will pay more for it. If you don't care about toilet style, we can cross fancy toilets off the list."

I didn't want to think about toilets at all, let alone toilet fashion, so we eliminated the stylish toilets.

"Lastly, we have to think about space," said my salesperson. "Some folks have a small space for a toilet, so we have toilets where the tank fits in the wall, saving a lot of space. The downside is, if something breaks, you may have to bust into the wall to fix it."

I've got a pretty big bathroom, so I eliminated the space-saving yet difficult-to-maintain toilets. We were down to three toilets! "So, which one would you pick?" I asked.

The salesperson said, "Look, I gotta come clean here. I work for Toto, so I'm going to recommend the Toto toilet, but you would be fine with any of those toilets. Personally, I would pick the Toto toilet anyway. You can go online and read the reviews. Everyone loves this toilet, and it's got the best quality rating of the three. It costs a bit more than the others, but if you just want to buy a toilet and never think about toilets again, that's the one I would pick."

I paid for the Toto toilet, and I was done. Start to finish, I had spent fifteen minutes in the store.

Buyers Want a Guide

What happened there? Was the salesperson giving me a pushy hard sell on a toilet? No. Was the salesperson giving me a walkthrough of every feature a toilet could have? Nope. What he did was give me a way to categorize all of my options so I could make an informed choice for myself based on what was most important to me. He was acting like a knowledgeable guide, and in doing so, he taught me how to confidently make a purchase.

I believe that for any considered purchase, we can create a pitch, in the form of a story or narrative, that teaches customers how to buy. Not only that, but I also believe that we can create a narrative that helps our best-fit customers easily understand why they should choose us and feel very confident in making that decision.

The Typical B2B Software Purchase

As a vendor, we often don't stop to think about the process a buyer goes through to purchase our product. Let's look at how a typical B2B software product is purchased.

One morning, Janet, a chief financial officer, wakes up, and she's worried. The company is going through an audit and the team is struggling to get it done using their current accounting system, which was never designed for companies that worry about regulatory reporting. She decides the company needs to switch accounting systems. Does Janet start looking at accounting packages herself? No way—she's too busy, and there's the audit to deal with. She assigns the job to Joey, her director of finance operations, to figure it out. Joey is simultaneously annoyed and petrified. He doesn't know anything about state-of-the-art accounting systems. Sure, he's used the one they have, and a different product at his previous job, but who knows what else is out there? He knows they need better auditing capabilities, but what else should he be looking out for? Joey knows this purchase is going to take some effort.

The Buyer Is Overwhelmed

Joey decides to do some research first. He googles "accounting software" and gets 685 million results. He clicks on an article called "Best Accounting Software for Small Businesses" and gets a list of more than a dozen packages. He finds a few comparison sites with names like TrustRadius, Capterra, and G2 that each list dozens of alternatives. The top lists all contain different vendors. He finds industry analysts like Gartner and Forrester Research, which also have their own lists of top accounting packages, and again there are different vendors on each list. Joey starts to look at vendor websites. Each vendor claims to be an award-winning leader and each site includes quotes from happy customers and glowing reviews.

The Sales Rep Isn't Helping
the Buyer Make a Decision

Eventually, Joey narrows down the choices to a shortlist of vendors. He might sign up for free versions or trials for each of the vendors on his list, but he's still not sure yet exactly what he needs, so he sets up sales appointments with each vendor. Each meeting turns out to be exactly the same. The call starts with the sales rep asking questions about Joey's company and its requirements for accounting software. Joey answers as best he can, but the truth is, he isn't entirely sure his list of requirements is correct or complete. The rep then switches gears and gives Joey a demo of the product. Joey feels like he has been invited to step into a wind tunnel of features. He doesn't understand many of them, but all seem potentially important for his company. By the end of the product walkthrough, Joey's feeling of overwhelm is peaking.

The Buyer Is Nervous
Because the Stakes Are High

Joey knows he is going to have to get IT and a few end users involved at some point before he can make a recommendation to Janet, and he's worried a poor choice might make him look stupid. If the product isn't a great fit, the company might be impacted, and that's not good. Joey might get passed over for his next promotion or, worse, fired.

The Safest Choice Is the Easiest Choice

If you're a buyer like Joey, what's the easiest decision to make at this point? The easiest decision would be to go back to Janet and recommend the company sticks with the current solution. Hey, it's been working fine for years, it should be

The easiest, safest purchase decision is often no decision.

okay for a couple more, and besides, there is that audit to deal with right now. Maybe next year someone can look into getting new software. "Someone," he thinks, "that isn't me." So, the company does nothing.

"Do Nothing" Is Your Fiercest Competitor

You might believe that the decision to do nothing happens infrequently, but you would be mistaken. In their 2022 book, *The JOLT Effect: How High Performers Overcome Customer Indecision*, Matthew Dixon and Ted McKenna reveal that between 40 and 60 percent of purchase processes end in no decision. Interestingly, most of the time, this doesn't mean that the buyer has decided their current solution is better than the alternatives. Instead, the buyer doesn't feel confident they have the information needed to make an informed choice. The worry that they could make a costly mistake leads them to dropping out of the purchase process completely. Customers can't figure out how they should evaluate and buy solutions, so they simply don't buy anything.

Not making a purchase at all is an incredibly attractive option for a buyer who is worried about making a poor choice. A buyer won't get in trouble for simply suggesting the company keep doing what they are doing. Hey, it's not perfect, but it's been working more or less okay for years. Why not wait and hang on for another year (or another, or another after that)? Nobody has to go through the pain of training and learning a new system. Nobody gets mad because the new system didn't do what was promised. Moving away from a solution that kinda, sorta does the job takes more than effort—it also takes courage. As vendors, we underestimate the pull of "no decision" at our peril.

It's also important to understand that when a customer fails to make a decision, this doesn't always signal a strong preference for their current solution. No decision is as likely to be a vote against change as it is a vote for the status quo. As a vendor, you always need to position against the buyer's status quo, even if there are other vendors to worry about on the customer's shortlist. Part of positioning against the status quo is making the case for change.

Now more than ever, buyers have access to mountains of information—from vendors, review sites, and analysts—but they struggle to make sense of it. It is a mistake to assume that because such information exists, buyers no longer need any help to make a purchase decision. The effort to make sense of that information is massive. Buyers are drowning in information but starved for market insight. Prospects who can't confidently make a choice between options will generally take the lowest risk option, which is to simply do nothing and keep using the status quo.

Emotions in B2B Selling

Consumer marketers talk a lot about the role of emotions in the purchase process. Many of the personal purchases we make are driven by our feelings and desires related to self-worth, acceptance, status, love, and good old-fashioned sex. Emotions matter in business purchases, too, but the types of emotions that drive purchase behaviors are often different. Fear is the granddaddy of B2B emotions. Fear of failure. Fear of the repercussions of making a poor decision. Fear of looking stupid. Fear of getting fired. In a sales situation, invoking feelings like trust and confidence can go a long way toward helping buyers overcome their fear. Later in the book, I will talk more about how you can build trust and confidence in your buyer.

WHAT DO CUSTOMERS WANT FROM VENDORS?

· · · · · · · · · · · · · · · · · · · ·

So, what should your role be in helping your customers make purchase decisions?

Many of the technology start-ups I work with assume that helping customers buy isn't really their job as vendors. Their job is to sell their product. They assume that customers can and will do their own research, figure out their purchase criteria, make a shortlist, evaluate the options, and choose a product to purchase. They believe the vendor's job is to understand customers' problems and show how their solution solves them. Many companies are convinced that buyers don't want to hear their opinions on how customers should make a purchase decision. And besides, why would the customer believe them?

But as it turns out, customers want more from vendors than they generally give them. In the groundbreaking 2011 book *The Challenger Sale*, authors Matthew Dixon and Brent Adamson reveal that buyers placed the most value on a sales rep's teaching skills. They found that the key characteristics of a world-class sales experience all related to the sales rep's ability to help customers figure out how to make an informed purchase. Research tells us that in a sales call, buyers expect sellers to help them understand their options. Buyers would like vendors to help them understand the trade-offs between different approaches to solving their problem. They want to understand potential pitfalls and how to avoid them. Buyers are looking for ways to understand what choices are available to them and how they should choose between them. This stands in stark contrast to what many companies are currently communicating across marketing and sales.

Often, we simply aren't giving buyers what they want. Go to most technology companies' websites or talk to their sales reps and you won't hear anything about the market or competitors. They are talking about the company and the product in complete isolation. You may be highlighting what you believe your best features are, but you are leaving it up to the customer to determine why those features matter and whether or not other alternatives can accomplish the same thing. Buyers are left doing all the work to figure out what is important and what isn't, and how different vendors stack up for businesses like theirs.

The person leading a B2B purchase process is tasked with making a well-informed, low-risk, defensible purchase decision. Vendors tend to assume the question the prospect wants them to answer is, "Why pick you?" Instead, the question the customer really wants the vendor to answer is, "Why pick you over all the alternatives?" If the vendor really wants to answer that latter question, they need to go beyond talking about their product and its features in isolation.

Buyers Are Experts in Pain, Vendors Are Experts in Solutions

Marketing and salespeople are often taught that customers have all the answers. Marketers are taught that any good marketing effort starts with customer research. Salespeople are taught that a good sales call starts with asking the customer questions about their situation, pain points, and goals.

Knowing your customers is vitally important. You need to deeply understand what motivates them, and the jobs they need to accomplish, and you can understand that only by talking to your customers because they are experts in their pain. After a purchase, customers can tell you a lot about how they are using your product and what they love and hate about your solution. Customers can also tell you what other solutions they evaluated and, if you are good at pulling this out of them, why they chose you.

But customers don't understand the market the way you do. As vendors operating in this solution space, you are more knowledgeable about what is possible and what isn't. You understand the underlying technology, and what its potential is, much better than your prospects do.

Understanding the solution space in which you operate *is* your business. Every day, everyone in the company is thinking and learning about and working on this. Customers are focused on their own businesses, and they don't start thinking about your market until they are in a purchase process. And often the person in charge of making a purchase recommendation has never purchased a product like yours before.

SO HOW should all of this be reflected in a sales pitch? Let's look at a specific example that shows the difference between a traditional product walkthrough–style pitch and one that is designed to help customers buy.

A SALES PITCH STORY: HELP SCOUT

HELP SCOUT launched their customer service platform in 2011, a time when the market for software to support customers was already crowded with competition, including Zendesk, already a well-funded, fast-growing leader in the space.

Help Scout was built with a different attitude toward customer service. Traditional vendors viewed support as a cost center and developed solutions to help drive down costs by reducing the time spent with agents and driving customers to low-cost self-serve channels. Help Scout was built with more modern online businesses in mind. In businesses that don't have stores or salespeople, customer support is one of the few places where customers directly interact with the company. For these businesses, the experience a customer has in support has the potential to strengthen a customer's loyalty to the brand and drive repeat purchases and revenue growth.

Help Scout's customers have many options when looking for customer service software. For many of these customers, the status quo is simply using a shared email inbox for support. But as their business grows, so does their need for advanced support features like prioritization and assignments. That leads them to look at traditional help desk vendors. Those platforms have plenty of advanced support features but are more difficult to use and were designed for cost reduction, not for giving customers a great experience that leads to loyalty and growth for the business.

Why a features-only pitch for Help Scout doesn't work.
Many SaaS (software as a service) businesses like Help
Scout would merely give a prospect a tour of their features.
This product walkthrough–style demo would simply sound
like a tour of Help Scout's features—show the shared inbox
interface, show how multiple inboxes are set up, show the
integrated knowledge base, show how to avoid duplicate
replies, show automated workflows, show integrations with
other apps, etc. Would this demo help a customer make a
purchase decision? No, it wouldn't. Many of these features
seem to overlap with either a shared inbox or traditional help
desk software. How is Help Scout really different, and what
value can it deliver that other solutions can't? The feature
pitch doesn't answer these questions.

**What would a sales pitch that helps customers buy look
like?** Instead of a traditional product walkthrough, Help
Scout helps customers understand their point of view on the
market and how their approach is different from the alternatives. It then moves to a demo focused on the value that only
they can deliver. The conversation goes something like this:

REP: We've seen with the digital brands we work with that
customer service is an effective way to build brand loyalty
and drive growth. Great service can decrease customer
acquisition costs and drive customer referrals.

PROSPECT: We certainly think great service is important for
our business.

REP: We've seen companies like yours start with a shared inbox, which is easy for service folks to use. Eventually, however, the business grows, and they start looking for more scalable support features like workflows and assignments. How have you folks been handling support so far?

PROSPECT: We use a shared inbox today, but we have a hard time handling the volume of requests we get, so we are looking for something more scalable.

REP: Many of our customers will then look at traditional help desk software. Those solutions have advanced features, but they do have some drawbacks. They're difficult to use compared to a shared inbox, but more importantly, the products were designed to reduce support costs by driving customers to low-cost channels and reducing the number of support tickets. They do this at the expense of delivering a great customer experience.

PROSPECT: We're worried about how hard it will be to get our service reps up to speed with a help desk package. We certainly want to ensure we are giving customers a great experience.

REP: We believe the perfect customer service solution for companies like yours would be as easy to use as a shared inbox, have the advanced features you need so you don't grow out of it, and be highly focused on delivering an amazing customer service experience. Would you agree with that?

PROSPECT: That's what we are looking for.

REP: Great, let me show you how Help Scout does this.

At this point, the rep moves to a demo that is organized around their key value points:

- An easy-to-use inbox experience: showing the key points of the user interface (UI)

- Advanced support features you won't outgrow: showing workflows, assignments, etc.

- Delivering a great customer experience—customer chooses their preferred channel, customers are never assigned a ticket number, etc.

Unlike a traditional product walkthrough, this pitch makes it perfectly clear how Help Scout is different and better than the alternatives. It gives customers a view of the entire market and helps them understand where Help Scout fits. It also allows sales to show the product but keeps the focus on the value only they can deliver.

PART TWO

SALES PITCH PRINCIPLES

Before we look at how to structure a sales pitch, let's go over what needs to happen before and during a first sales call with a prospect.

For some readers, these sales concepts are obvious, but understanding these elements and how they fit into your sales pitch can mean the difference between winning and losing. These key elements are qualification, discovery, product demonstrations, and differentiated value.

Qualification

The process of qualification is making sure your prospect is a potential good fit for your offering. Qualification is important because you don't want to waste critical sales resources (not to mention the customer's time!) pitching a product to a company that isn't a fit for what you do.

Qualification criteria can be a range of things depending on your product and the way you sell. Criteria could include information like company size or revenue, whether there is a technical fit for your solution, and the company's budget, for example.

For most companies selling to businesses, qualification happens before the buyer gets to a first true sales meeting. Some companies will do this online with a questionnaire or form, but more often, business development reps (BDRs) will have a short call with a prospect to qualify them, and only those who meet the qualification criteria will be booked for a first call with a sales rep.

The sales pitch is the story you tell in that first call, so the prospect you are talking to should already be qualified. If your sales process doesn't include a qualification step before a first call, you will need to work qualification questions into your discovery conversation.

Discovery

Discovery usually happens in a first sales call. Done well, discovery is a conversation during which the buyer teaches the seller about their pain, problems, and situation, but the seller is also teaching the buyer about their point of view on problems and solutions in the space.

A successful discovery conversation aligns buyers and sellers on the true nature of the problem, what to consider when evaluating solutions, and the value a perfect solution should deliver. That means a good sales pitch needs to accommodate space for a rep to have a discovery conversation with a prospect.

Product Demonstrations

I have never encountered a prospect who wants to be "sold" to. Nobody wants to be on the receiving end of pushy, high-pressure tactics that try to force them into making a decision they aren't comfortable with. So I strongly believe that when a prospect comes to your site and clicks the button that says, "Book a demo," what they crave most is knowledge that spans both the market and your product. Prospects want to understand how to make a good choice that doesn't get them fired. Yes, they want to see the product, but they also want insight to help them make sense of what they are looking at.

Many, but not all, companies do a product demonstration in a first call with a customer. Often, prospects book the sales meeting explicitly because they want to see a demo and get a feel for the experience your product delivers. In some cases, demonstrating how your product works is the best way to communicate the value of what it does.

There are various structures for product demos. The most used one I've seen is a "product walkthrough." This is simply a guided tour of the key functionality of the product. I've seen other variations, including a "day in the life" demo that shows how a user would complete typical tasks. Some companies prefer to do a highly customized demo, tailored to what they believe the customer wants to see.

When You Do a Product Demo, Always Show Your Best

No matter what format you choose for your product demonstration, a first call should show customers the best of what you can do, whether or not they requested to see what you would consider your best capabilities. As I showed earlier, buyers aren't always exactly sure what their purchase criteria should be. A first demo is a chance to firmly position yourself in the prospect's mind by showing what makes your product different and better than the alternatives in general.

It is impossible to differentiate yourself without addressing the alternatives.

For example, I worked at a company that sold a customer relationship management (CRM) solution for investment banks, and we had a unique killer feature that delivered value that investment bankers loved. Did any of our prospects ask to see that capability in a qualification call? Never. They didn't know it was even possible. Did we show it to every customer anyway? You bet we did, and it was the main reason we won business.

If You Customize Your Demo, Do It in a Second Call

Some companies want to do a customized demo. In my opinion, that can generally come in a second meeting. It's difficult to customize a demo until after you've done discovery, and showing a completely customized demo in the first meeting misses an opportunity to show prospects what you can do, beyond what they already think they need. A custom demo can come in a follow-up meeting if that makes sense.

You Can Skip a Demo in Some Instances

I also think it's fine to skip doing a demo in a first sales call. Sometimes, customers have already done a trial or used a free version of the product and they simply don't need to see it. Other times, there simply isn't much value in showing the product in isolation. For example, I worked at a company that sold databases and we rarely demoed the product (hey, if you've seen one SQL query, you've seen them all). Instead, we focused on ensuring that our prospects conceptually understood the capabilities that enabled us to deliver unique business value.

Differentiated Value

Value, and more importantly differentiated value, is at the core of great sales and marketing. Yet, of all the concepts in marketing and sales, value is probably the least understood. More than anything else you might learn in this book, if you learn that a great sales pitch should be oriented around your differentiated value, I guarantee you will sell more.

Many of us working in technology come from a technical background, and it isn't surprising that most start-ups will naturally focus on features in their sales and marketing. It's our comfort zone. But as much as we love features, what really matters for customers is the business value they get from those features.

For many features of B2B products, you cannot assume that customers can make the leap from features to why the features matter. Value is the answer to the question, "So what?"

- Your database supports advanced usage metrics, including query runs. So what? So support personnel can better assist customers.

- Your CRM automatically sends status updates to managers. So what? So your sales reps can spend less time building reports and more time selling.

- Your accounting system supports adding an expiration date on inventory items. So what? So you can ensure you never sell an expired item and can easily know when to apply discounts to items that expire soon.

In a B2B sales situation, beyond simply the value you can deliver, you win deals based on your **differentiated** value—the value you can deliver that no other alternative can. It may be true, for example, that your product saves time for companies. But what if all your competitors also help companies save time? Suddenly, your value is interesting but not a reason to buy.

Exposing your differentiated value, and helping a prospect understand why it is important for them, is the key to winning business. A great sales pitch tells the story of the value that only your product can deliver and why that value is very important to a certain kind of buyer. It is the answer to the question, "Why pick us over the alternatives?"

You Can't Differentiate Yourself without Addressing the Alternatives

You cannot teach customers your differentiated value and why it matters without talking about the alternatives in the market. A good sales pitch addresses the alternatives and helps customers understand how to categorize them, and what their strengths and weaknesses are for different types of buyers. In the upcoming chapters, I will describe how to determine your differentiated value if you aren't certain what it is. I will also cover how to orient your sales pitch around the unique value only you can deliver.

BEFORE I jump into what makes a good sales pitch, let's look at the narrative frameworks that exist today and what they can teach us about storytelling for sales.

FOUR COMMON APPROACHES TO STORYTELLING IN A SALES PITCH

If you believe that your job as a vendor is to teach customers how to confidently make a purchase decision, then how do you do that?

Smart businesses tell a wide range of stories for different audiences and to sell different things.

For example, many companies have an **"employer" story** designed to help prospective employees decide if they should join the company. This story is often focused on the company's values and mission.

If a company is raising money, they will use an **investor pitch** to help investors understand why they are a good investment. This story is often focused on the company vision and the business they will be in five or ten years in the future.

And then there is the **sales pitch** that sells a product or service. Unlike the investor pitch, which is all about the future, an effective sales pitch is firmly oriented in the present. This is the story that companies tell prospects to answer the question, "Why choose us over the alternatives you could choose today?"

Naturally, these different sales stories are also structured differently. Most sales and marketing teams use one of four distinct approaches to craft a narrative or pitch:

1 The product walkthrough
2 The problem/solution pitch
3 The vision narrative
4 The hero's journey

Each approach has pros and cons, depending on the audience and what you are trying to achieve with the pitch. Let's dive in.

The Product Walkthrough

I have spent most of my career running marketing teams at technology start-ups. In almost every case, the structure the sales team used in a first sales meeting was essentially a product walkthrough. Some walkthroughs simply click through each menu item and explain what it does. Others describe how a user would accomplish certain tasks. Some do a more customized walkthrough based on what they know about the prospect.

When Does It Work Best?
This style of narrative works best when the buyer is highly educated or the solution they are using now is very similar to what you sell. Buyers in this situation will be better able to translate the features they are shown into business value.

What's the Downside?
It is focused on features, not value. Prospects don't necessarily understand why they should care about particular features, so they may not be able to figure out why those features are important for their business.

"Identify stories that pique buyers' curiosity and move them to action."

JILL KONRATH

You spend too much time on capabilities that are not differentiating. Most product walkthroughs try to show everything they can do without highlighting what is differentiated. Is the way you log in innovative? Is how you set up an account any different from the alternatives? What value is there in showing that? The product walkthrough generally does a poor job of answering the question, "Why pick you over the alternatives?"

The product walkthrough is all about your solution and leaves no room to discuss the market. The product walkthrough does not accomplish what most B2B buyers want: a way to understand all the alternatives so they can confidently make the right choice for their business. To confidently choose you, buyers need to understand why the alternatives can't meet their needs better.

It leaves no room for discovery. Most product walkthroughs don't have a natural place for a rep to have a discovery conversation.

The Problem/Solution Pitch

The problem/solution pitch is generally very similar to the product walkthrough pitch with bit of setup before you jump into the demo. In these pitches, you describe "the problem" the customer has and then position your product as "the solution" to that problem, before following up with a demo that shows how you deliver the solution.

When Does It Work Best?
Like the product walkthrough, this style of narrative works best when the buyer is highly educated and can translate the

features they are shown into business value. This style of pitch is also more effective when the only competitor in the market is the status quo. It is dramatically less effective when there are many alternatives for the prospect to consider.

What's the Downside?

Your competitors define the problem the same way you do. You have identified that folks looking for accounting software need a fast, easy way to do accounting. That's obvious, and all your competitors also solve that problem. There is nothing in this pitch style that gives you a way to highlight your differentiated value and answer the question, "Why pick you over the alternatives?"

It is focused on features, not your differentiated value. The problem/solution pitch tends to turn into a feature walkthrough once the problem has been defined. There is no focus on the value you can deliver that the other alternatives cannot.

This pitch is all about your solution and leaves no room to discuss the market. Much like the product walkthrough, the problem/solution pitch does not give buyers a way to understand all the alternatives so they can confidently make the right choice for their business.

The Vision Narrative

In technology companies that are raising money, the CEO will have a narrative that is used to pitch the company to investors. This narrative structure is often formed around describing the current approach to a particular problem (the tired and crappy "old way"), and then painting a picture of an alternative

"You can't sell anything if you can't tell anything."

BETH COMSTOCK

approach (the amazing and shiny "new way") that, if current trends continue, will be a much better way to do things in the future. The vision narrative is less about the current state of the product and more about its future state and the company's strategy to get there.

When Does It Work Best?

The vision narrative works best when pitching investors. For investors, the vision pitch does a good job of explaining where the company is going and why you are a good potential investment.

What's the Downside?

It ignores competitors beyond the status quo. For most solutions, there are many alternatives a customer might consider. Attempting to position a wide range of alternatives as "the old way" simply doesn't work when there are competing "new ways" to consider, as well as alternatives that cannot be credibly classified as simply "old" or "new."

The vision narrative gives buyers yet another reason to delay a decision. Even if you successfully sell the vision, you risk giving the buyer a reason to delay a purchase. There's no urgency to buy something when it doesn't exist yet, not to mention the added risk that you may never deliver on the vision. Prospects on the receiving end of a vision pitch often respond with, "Hey, that's great. Come back next year and pitch this to me when it exists!"

It isn't centered on differentiated value. It assumes that "new" is valuable (and the only value that matters). For B2B buyers, newness isn't always obviously valuable. Worse, it can have negative associations—untested, unreliable, lacking in features, or insecure. The vision narrative is not oriented around differentiated value—what your solution can do for their business that no other solution can—which is the core of any good sales pitch.

The Hero's Journey

The most famous narrative structure for storytelling in general is known as the "hero's journey." The hero's journey starts with a hero who goes on an adventure or quest, learns a lesson, uses that knowledge to achieve victory, and then returns home transformed. This story structure is widely used in entertainment, so much so that the most common example of this structure is the plot for the movie *Star Wars*.

Many marketers have been introduced to a version of this storytelling structure through the work of Donald Miller and his book *Building a StoryBrand*, which teaches marketers how to use elements of the hero's journey to build marketing messaging. The StoryBrand structure moves through seven steps: The **hero** (the customer) has a **problem** and meets a **guide** (you!), who gives the hero a **plan** and calls them to **action**. This action ends in **success** and helps the hero avoid **failure**. The thing I like the most is that this structure makes it completely clear that as a vendor, your role is to be a guide, helping the hero (the buyer) achieve success and avoid failure.

When Does It Work Best?

The hero's journey is used when the primary goal is to entertain and engage your customer through a story. It's a structure that works well for content like customer case studies, where your goal is to tell the story of a customer's journey from having had a problem, to choosing you to solve that problem, to experiencing success afterward.

What's the Downside?

"The plan" is focused on execution, not on how to decide what action to take. In Miller's book, the hero (the customer) encounters the guide (you), who gives them a plan. One of the sample plans provided includes these three steps: 1) download the software, 2) integrate your database into the system, and 3) revolutionize your customer interaction. This is the answer to "How do I get started?," not a plan to help a customer understand why to choose you. Prospects need help understanding their options and how to make a confident decision.

The concept of alternatives is missing. The core of a good sales narrative is a rubric for helping a customer make choices. The hero's journey structure doesn't focus on the step that a prospect is primarily concerned with in a sales situation: "How do I confidently choose between seemingly similar options?"

ALTHOUGH THE narrative structures we've just explored may serve you well for recruitment, raising capital, or crafting a customer case study, they aren't well suited to a sales situation. So, what should a narrative structure for selling look like?

THE ROAD TO A BETTER SALES PITCH STRUCTURE

Looking at the gaps in the other storytelling structures can teach us something about what is needed to build a great sales pitch.

I'd like to start by explaining where the ideas for this structure came from, how it's been tested, and how it's evolved over time.

I began my career in start-ups as a product marketer for an enterprise software start-up, and my responsibilities included helping craft a pitch deck, demo, and script for the sales team to use in first meetings with qualified prospects.

I inherited a sales pitch deck that had this structure:

1 It started with an "about us" slide that listed the year we were founded, the current number of employees, and the money we had raised.

2 Following that was a busy slide full of customer logos (affectionately referred to as "the NASCAR slide").

3 We then moved to a "problem" slide, which stated the problem our product was designed to solve. We generally defined this problem at a high level, exactly the way every one of our competitors defined it.

4 Then came the demo, which was a product feature walk-through. We showed the prospect how to log on and get started, walked them through the main menus, and showed how their common tasks would be completed. Most of the time was spent here.

5 We wrapped up with a high-level pricing slide.

We never built a sales pitch deck from scratch. We modified pitches that seemed to have existed since the dawn of time itself. Nobody questioned the flow or structure of the pitch or the demo. We simply did it the way we always did it.

What Happens to Positioning When a Prospect Moves from Marketing to Sales?

As my career progressed, I became a VP of marketing, and I started to notice that although we obsessed over the story we were telling in our marketing campaigns and materials, when customers made it to a sales meeting, there was no storytelling or positioning happening at all. Our positioning defined how our product was special and different from anything else in the market, but our sales pitch rarely reflected that positioning. Once leads got passed to the sales team, they weren't hearing that story. Instead, they were hit with a barrage of features and a bit of information about our company history. This seemed like an incredible missed opportunity to me, even if I wasn't sure exactly what to do about it yet.

Discovering the Magic of Pitching a Unique Point of View

Fast-forward a couple of years to when I was at IBM launching a new software product. Part of getting ready for the launch involved my team creating a first-call deck with a demo and a script for the sales team. Unsurprisingly, IBM had a very long, detailed process for creating this material, which my boss delivered to my desk in the form of a four-inch-thick binder.

Like many things I encountered at IBM, at first this procedure seemed like an exercise in useless process overkill designed to test both my patience and my tolerance for unnecessary bullcrap. And after running through the process, I still felt that way about most of the binder's contents. However, there were a handful of pages that opened my eyes to some things I had never thought about doing in a sales pitch.

The most interesting thing to me about the IBM pitch structure was the way these pitches started. The conversation never began with a discussion about the company or the product. Instead, it always started with a discussion about IBM's point of view on the market. Reps would talk about what IBM perceived to be important considerations for companies looking at any solution in the market. They would then discuss how different approaches to providing a solution stacked up. Reps were doing discovery at this step, but also giving the customers a big picture of the entire market and teaching them how to make informed choices. The sales reps were skillfully positioning our product in the minds of customers, relative to the competition, and that was winning us deals.

"Stop selling. Start helping."

ZIG ZIGLAR

Applying the Lessons Learned

When I left IBM, I went back to work for another start-up as the VP of marketing. I worked on shifting the company's positioning, and soon after that the company hired a new VP of sales. Together, we decided to tackle recreating the first-call sales deck and demo to better reflect the new positioning.

I hauled out the binder I had conveniently "borrowed" from IBM and highlighted the set of things in the structure that I thought might work for us. In particular, I wanted to see if we could develop a "setup" phase to our pitch that would help our sales reps position our product in a way that mirrored how we were positioning it in marketing. We also restructured the demo to focus on our differentiated value as opposed to what it was: a contextless product walkthrough.

We rolled the new pitch out to the sales team, and in a few months, we were on a path to doubling revenue for the year. Before the year was out, we were acquired by IBM, a great outcome for the company while also conveniently giving me a way to return their property and avoid being sent to binder-stealer jail.

Battle Testing the Sales Pitch Structure

After that experience, I worked at a series of start-ups, and in each one we recreated the sales pitch deck using an evolving version of this new sales pitch structure. As an in-house VP of marketing, and working with my counterpart in sales, I used the structure to build a dozen or so sales pitches. Each time, the structure worked and we saw sales grow.

I switched to consulting work with a focus on positioning. Part of any positioning work I do with a company involves creating a new sales pitch that reflects the company's positioning. I've used this structure to translate new positioning into a sales pitch with over two hundred technology companies—from small, early-stage start-ups, to companies on the cusp of going public, to some of the largest technology companies in the world. The structure is thoroughly battle-tested, so I know where it works (and some cases where it doesn't) and the strengths and weaknesses of this approach. I've taught dozens of courses on how to build a pitch, and now I'm going to teach it to you. Let's start with the basic components.

THE
SALES PITCH
STRUCTURE

. . . .

The goal of a great sales pitch is to help customers understand all their choices, the trade-offs between each, and when to pick your solution.

That means a great sales pitch should:

1 Help prospects understand the entire market, including other common alternatives beyond your product and the pros and cons of those alternatives mapped to their particular situation.

2 Accommodate the salesperson's need to do in-depth discovery.

3 Help prospects clearly understand your differentiated value versus other alternatives and why the unique value only you can deliver is critically important.

4 Accommodate a product demonstration (should you choose to do one) as a natural part of the narrative flow of the pitch.

5 Include a clear call to action for what the prospect should do next.

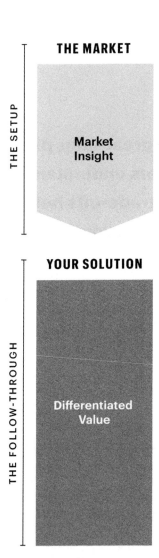

Figure 1

To accomplish this, I've broken the sales pitch structure into two distinct phases: the **setup** and the **follow-through**.

1 The setup focuses on offering your insights about the market, competitive alternatives, and discovery.

2 The follow-through focuses on your solution for the customer or, more specifically, on the value that only your product can deliver, including a demo (if you want one), and ends with a call to action.

At a high level, the sales pitch looks like this (see Figure 1).

The Setup

The setup is where you have a conversation with the prospect about the market. Specifically, this is when you teach prospects the market context they need to know to understand the importance of the value only you can deliver. It makes sense to do this before you talk about your differentiated value.

The setup consists of three distinct components: **Insight**, **Alternatives**, and **The Perfect World**.

1 **Insight:** The insight frames the conversation by starting with what your experience has taught you about the customer's situation, problems, and the solutions in the market. This critically important step points the customer toward what they need to know to understand why your differentiated value is important to them.

2 **Alternatives:** In this step, you discuss what alternative solutions exist in the market today, and the pros and cons

of those alternatives for various customers. This is a conversational step, and where you will do discovery. The goal of this step is to help paint a picture of the market for prospects while simultaneously getting a better understanding of the prospect's current situation.

3 **The Perfect World:** This step outlines the characteristics of a perfect solution for your target customers. To arrive here, you draw on the discussion about the alternatives in the previous step, as guided by the insight introduced in the first step.

The Follow-Through

At this point, your sales pitch will transition from the setup to the follow-through. The follow-through is focused primarily on exposing the value only your product can deliver to the prospect. This section has five distinct components.

1 **The Introduction:** You introduce the company and the product. This is how you will navigate the transition from the setup part of the sales pitch. Usually, this is also the place where you introduce your definition of the market category you position yourself in.

2 **Differentiated Value:** In this step, you cover the value that only your product can deliver for a specific customer and the features that enable that value, which is often (but not always) done with a demo. This step is the meatiest part of the sales pitch and where you will likely spend most of your time in a first call with a prospect.

THE MARKET

THE SETUP

Insight

Alternatives

Perfect World

YOUR SOLUTION

THE FOLLOW-THROUGH

Introduction

Value

Proof

Objections

Ask

Figure 2

3 **Proof:** Now you need to show how you can deliver the value you say you can. This can take the form of case studies, awards, third-party validation, and other proof points.

4 **Objections (optional):** This is an optional step in the sales pitch where you explicitly handle common objection you believe are critical to address before the end of the meeting. This may range from concerns about how difficult it is to adopt the solution, integration, or pricing concerns.

5 **The Ask:** You finish the meeting by recommending a next step for the prospect.

The full process looks like this (see Figure 2).

To help you out with this, there are templates and other reference materials at **aprildunford.com/books**.

PART
THREE

A GREAT SALES PITCH STARTS WITH SOLID POSITIONING

· ·

A good sales pitch doesn't begin with a blank sheet of paper. You need to gather a distinct set of inputs before you start. A great sales pitch will be a story rooted in your positioning.

Before you build a sales pitch, you need to review your positioning. When you think about your current positioning, you may or may not be happy with it. But your sales pitch will reflect your positioning, and as my university coding professor used to say, garbage in, garbage out.

If your positioning is weak, the sales pitch is going to be weak. As you work through building a sales pitch, you might find that some of your positioning components are not particularly well defined. If that's the case, I highly recommend getting your team together to review your positioning. (As I mentioned in the introduction, I wrote a book about how you might want to do that, so I would suggest starting there!)

In marketing, positioning defines your differentiated value and the target buyer for your message. Your sales story should reflect that same narrative, so it makes sense that you should start with your positioning when constructing a sales pitch.

In the following sections, I'm going to give you a high-level overview of the components of positioning and how they map to the sections of the sales pitch.

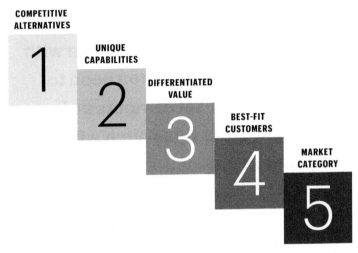

Figure 3

The Five Components of Positioning

Let's look at the five components of positioning and how they relate to each other (see Figure 3).

1   **Competitive Alternatives:** These are the alternative ways of solving the problem in the minds of customers. This could include whatever the status quo solution is. For B2B technology, that might include things like Microsoft Excel, manual processes, or "hire an intern to do it."

2 **Unique Capabilities:** These are the capabilities of your offering that the alternatives do not have. They can be traditional features of a product, as well as capabilities of the company such as professional services offerings or specialized expertise.

3 **Differentiated Value:** This is the value your product enables for customers. This could be something like "helps customers save money by reducing development costs" or "speeds time to market by streamlining operations."

4 **Best-Fit Customers:** This is the definition of a target account that is a good fit for your product. This usually includes firmographic information—for example, company size, revenue, number of employees—but it may also include other characteristics such as: the target account is already a Microsoft shop, or it has over one hundred gigabytes of internal data to be analyzed, or it has a distributed development team.

5 **Market Category:** The market category is the answer to the question, "What is it?" It's the context within which you position your product and serves as a starting point for customers to understand what your product is all about.

How the Positioning Components Work Together

All these positioning component pieces have a relationship with each other. In a typical positioning exercise, you work your way through the component pieces in a particular order.

1 You start with listing the competitive alternatives, or what customers would do if your solution didn't exist.

2 Once you have that list, your next question is, "What do we have that the alternatives do not?" The answers give you a list of differentiated or unique capabilities.

3 Then you can go down that list and ask, "*So what* for customers?" Put another way, "What is the value those capabilities enable for our buyers?"

4 Once you know what your differentiated value is, then you can figure out who your best-fit customers are. What are the characteristics of a target account that make them care a lot about the value only you can deliver?

5 In the final step, you identify your best market category. This is the context you position your product in so that your value is obvious to your target customers. This is the definition of the market you intend to win.

All these components will be critical inputs to the sales pitch. Let's look at an example of how this comes together.

A great sales pitch starts with great positioning.

A SALES PITCH STORY: LEVELJUMP

LEVELJUMP SOFTWARE (recently acquired by Salesforce) provides a sales enablement solution: it helps salespeople learn what they need to know to effectively sell the products they need to sell. To determine the company's positioning, let's work our way through the steps of the positioning process, starting with competitive alternatives and working through to market category.

1 **Competitive Alternatives:** Companies that buy LevelJump often start by putting sales material on a shared drive. As the sales teams grow, some of the companies will choose to use a content management system (or CMS) to manage materials and ensure that the folks on the sales team always have access to correct and current content. Some companies will decide to use a full-blown learning management system (or LMS) that allows them to create courses and curriculum and track which reps have taken which training.

2 **Unique Capabilities:** LevelJump is the only sales enablement solution built within Salesforce and can take full advantage of Salesforce data. (There is a longer list of other differentiated capabilities but, for the sake of keeping this example simple, I'm not going to list them all here.)

3 **Differentiated Value:** LevelJump is built on Salesforce. So what? So LevelJump can take advantage of sales data. So what? So we can measure the impact of sales enablement programs with sales metrics such as time to first deal and

time to make quota. So what? So we can track what is working and what isn't and improve sales enablement over time to ensure that sales reps are getting to the first deal and quota fulfillment faster, driving increased revenue for the business.

4 **Best-Fit Customers:** Companies hiring a lot of new sales reps (such as rapidly growing companies, companies that have recently taken on investment, and companies that have a high turnover in their sales teams) would care a great deal about this improvement in the time it takes to ramp up a new sales rep.

5 **Market Category:** In this case, LevelJump is clearly in the sales enablement space. If we wanted to get more specific or turn that category into more of a tagline, we could say: "sales enablement that drives results."

PREPARING YOUR POSITIONING BEFORE BUILDING A SALES PITCH

· ·

Since your positioning is a critical input, before starting the process to develop your sales pitch, you will want to document your positioning.

Each component of your positioning will need some preparation, so you are ready to map them to the components of the sales pitch. Let me show you how to capture your positioning so that it can be used as a starting point for the sales pitch.

What Are You Positioning and Pitching?

If you are a single-product company, then the focus of the sales pitch will be your product. If your company has multiple products, then the focus of the pitch will depend on your sales process and what you usually try to sell first to a new account.

Most multi-product companies I have worked with will give a prospect a full company pitch in a first sales call and do discovery to determine which individual products they should focus on beyond that conversation. There are exceptions to this rule, and sometimes you will want to focus on selling only a particular product, and then worry about up-selling or cross-selling the rest of the portfolio after you have landed the first deal. Regardless, if you are a multi-product company, it is very important to decide what you want to position in a first sales call before you build the pitch.

Who Is Your Audience?

When you are creating your positioning and building a sales pitch, you need to consider who you are aiming it at. In a typical B2B purchase decision, there are usually between five and eight people involved in that decision. So, do you need different positioning and a different pitch for each of them? The key is to figure out who is your champion.

In a typical technology purchase, you will encounter people in the following roles at some point in the purchase process:

- **The Economic Buyer.** This is the person who holds the budget and often has the ultimate approval over whether or not the purchase gets made.

- **The Champion.** The economic buyer is not always the person tasked with figuring out what product to buy. That job is often delegated to a person who is tasked with making a shortlist, doing an evaluation, getting buy-in from other stakeholders, and making a purchase recommendation to the economic buyer.

- **End Users.** End users will often be consulted in a purchase and may be involved in a proof of concept. They may not have the power to make a purchase decision but frequently have the power to stop a deal from happening if they don't like the product the champion is recommending. They are also critically important post-sale, particularly if you have a recurring revenue model.

- **IT Department.** Sometimes you are selling directly to the IT department, but often the budget for a technology purchase is held by a line of business (for example, sales, marketing, HR), and the evaluation happens primarily by those non-IT groups. In those cases, the IT department will often need to approve any technology purchase. Much like end users, if they are not the budget holders for the purchase, they don't get to make the final decision of what product to purchase, but they can stop a deal from happening if it doesn't meet their requirements for interoperability, manageability, or security, for example.

- **Legal and Purchasing.** If you sell to larger organizations, purchasing and legal teams might get involved in the latter stages of a deal. They don't usually get involved actively in the selection of a solution, but like other groups listed above, they do have the power to stop a purchase if it doesn't meet the company's legal or supplier agreement requirements.

Sell to Your Champion

As you can see from this list, each of these stakeholders will have different concerns. But you can also see that not all stakeholders are equally important in getting a deal done.

In the early stages of a purchase process, the champion matters much more than any other person. It's the champion who is doing the research to determine what the requirements are and making a shortlist. They are frequently the person

"How do you beat Bobby Fischer? You play him at any game but chess."

WARREN BUFFETT

sitting across from you in a first sales call. If you can't get the champion interested, you don't even get a chance to worry about all the other stakeholders because the champion is going to eliminate you from the process before they get those other groups involved. It is critical that your positioning and sales pitch are tuned to resonate for the champion if you want to be considered for a purchase.

That doesn't mean that the other stakeholders aren't important. As I mentioned, any one of those stakeholder groups holds the power to kill a sale at different points in the purchase process. You will need to worry about them, but that worry comes later. Once the champion has decided to consider your product as a potential solution, then a key part of your job is to understand the potential objections of all the other stakeholders and to arm the champion with the information to handle those objections.

Where and when you choose to manage the objections of the other stakeholders will depend on your sales process. For example, you might know that the IT department will have important security and management concerns. In a first pitch, you might touch on the fact that you understand and have dealt with those issues with other clients and can help both the champion and the IT group understand your approach, should you move forward with a deal. In other situations, you may not touch on objections of other groups in the initial sales pitch, but you are prepared to educate and arm the champion to have those conversations later in the sales process.

Your positioning and sales pitch need to resonate with the champion most. Worry about the other stakeholders once you have convinced the champion to consider you.

Determining and Documenting the Positioning Components

Once you are clear on what you are positioning and who the pitch is for, you can move on to documenting the component pieces of your positioning. These will be the key inputs to your sales pitch.

Competitive Alternatives

There are two main types of competitive alternatives: **status quo** and **direct.**

As the name suggests, status quo alternatives are the things your current customers were doing before they adopted your product. That could include using a spreadsheet, hiring an intern to do it, or even doing it manually with a pen and paper. This could also include using a legacy solution or functionality that is included in a software package, such as a CRM or accounting system, to get the job done. Direct alternatives are products that buyers put on a shortlist of solutions during a purchase process.

You don't need to position against competitors your prospects don't know about. You may know of companies that could compete against you, but the sales department never sees them land on a shortlist. If so, for now you don't have to worry about positioning against them. Although your product and strategy teams might want to keep an eye on these competitors as future threats, your marketing and sales teams can ignore them for now. If at some point you see these competitors show up in actual deals, you can adjust your positioning to handle them at that time.

Unique Capabilities

Once you have listed your true competitive alternatives, you can create a list of capabilities you have that the competitors don't. Capabilities include features of your product, but might also include capabilities of the company, such as your pricing model, professional services, or integration with other products in your portfolio. In the above LevelJump example, you can see that being built on Salesforce is a differentiated capability.

You can create this list by starting with your most common competitor and working down the list to the least common alternative. Differentiated capabilities might not be differentiated when compared to every alternative, and that's okay. Simply make a note of which competitor doesn't have that capability and move on.

Differentiated Value

The most critical component of your positioning is the value that only your product provides. Customers don't care that much about features; they care about what those features can enable for their business. You can determine the unique value your product delivers by going down the list of differentiated features and asking yourself, "So what? Why does a customer care about this feature? What value does this feature enable for a customer's business?"

As you move down your list, you will see value themes start to emerge, and you can cluster groups of features under the value theme they enable. That's a good thing. Customers can't digest and remember dozens of value points, so try to keep the number of value themes down to three or fewer.

Like capabilities, each value theme taken on its own might not be differentiating against every competitor. Taken together, however, you should be able to say that no other alternative can provide the combination of value that you can.

Your interpretation of your unique value is deeply informed by what you know about the good customers you already have, including their business situation, the job they want to get done with your product, and their business priorities. The more you understand that, the better job you will do in translating your unique features to value.

Best-Fit Customers

So now that you have determined the unique value you deliver to customers, the next question is, "Which customers care a lot about that value?" This step is where you list the characteristics of a target account that make them a good fit for what you do.

Typically, the characteristics of a target account will be a combination of firmographic characteristics of the company (for example, number of employees, revenue), but also characteristics that are more specific to the type of solution you are selling. These could include things like the number of employees in a particular department, or other technology platforms the company has already adopted, such as Amazon Web Services (AWS), Salesforce, or Microsoft Office.

When it comes to crafting a sales pitch, this step will help you understand who your audience is and where your marketing and sales teams should focus their efforts.

Market Category

You can think of the market category as the context you position your product in. The job of the market category is to serve as a starting point for prospects who don't know too much

An effective sales
pitch tells the story
of the business value
only you can deliver.

about your product. It is the simplified answer to the question, "What the heck is this thing?"

A good way to assess your market category is to look at your unique value and best-fit customers and ask, "Does this market category point best-fit customers toward my value or does it point them somewhere else?" In the case of LevelJump, we can see that sales enablement works for the company as a market category because it clearly points the prospect to the product's value (sales training that drives improved revenue).

Capture and Review Your Positioning

I like to recommend that teams document their positioning in a long-form file, where you can also capture relevant details about each component. Start-ups I work with like to summarize their positioning in a one-page format. I have used a template to do that, which you can download at **aprildunford .com/books**.

What If Your Product Hasn't Launched Yet?

If your product hasn't launched yet or is in the early stages with only a few paying customers, it's likely you won't know precisely what your positioning is. If that is the case, you can still work through the process of documenting your positioning and building a sales pitch to reflect it. However, that positioning should be treated like a "positioning thesis."

Your first wave of customers will help you validate your thesis. In my experience, you should expect your positioning to shift a lot as you learn more about which customers love your product and why. I recommend you keep your positioning a little loose as you work with your first wave of customers. Once you feel as though your positioning is validated with a group of paying customers, you can work to tighten it and the sales story that reflects it.

Positioning Will Change Over Time

Positioning is not a "set it and forget it" exercise. Your product's capabilities and its value will change over time. Your competitors are also upgrading their products, and things that are differentiators for you today might not be in the future. New competitors may enter the market, and others may exit. Customer preferences and spending priorities will also change over time.

I recommend you check in on your positioning a couple of times a year—and when there are changes in the landscape, differentiators, and buyer behavior, be prepared to adjust your position and the sales pitch to reflect where you are in the market.

Mapping Positioning
Components to the Sales Pitch

Each component of positioning maps to the components of the sales pitch. Some have a direct relationship; some are a combination of several components taken together. I will dive into more details about how exactly to map these components together as we go through how to build each of the steps of the sales pitch. But here is a quick overview of how this works.

1   **Insight:** This step in the sales pitch comes from a combination of your differentiated value and your best-fit customers. Insight represents the critical concepts your best-fit customers need to be aware of to understand why your unique value matters.

2   **Alternatives:** This step maps directly to the competitive alternatives you have captured in your positioning.

3   **The Perfect World:** The Perfect World step maps to your differentiated value. You can think of this step as a way of defining purchase criteria for the customers you sell to.

4   **The Introduction:** Here, you introduce the product using the market category from your positioning.

5   **Differentiated Value:** This maps directly to the differentiated value and unique capabilities from your positioning. This step in the sales pitch is all about demonstrating the value that only you can deliver and showing the features that enable that value.

6   **Proof:** This is the proof that you can deliver on the value you say you can.

7-8 **Objections and The Ask:** These two steps do not come from your positioning, but rather from your own sales experience and process.

NEXT, I WILL dive into each part of the pitch, including the details of how to map the components of your positioning to each step.

PART
FOUR

CONSTRUCTING THE SALES PITCH STORYBOARD

. . . .

Now that we have a structure and we understand the component pieces of positioning we need as inputs into the sales pitch, it's time to work on building a storyboard for the pitch.

Bringing a Team Together to Work on the Pitch

One big decision you'll need to make is whom to involve in building the sales pitch. I am a big believer in cross-functional team efforts for positioning and pitch development. In my experience, most weak positioning comes from misalignment across the team. Often, marketing and sales don't totally agree on what the differentiated value is, or product and sales don't see eye to eye on which competitors you need to position against. Founders can sometimes be focused so much on the future vision of the company that they lose sight of how to position the product as it exists today. Bringing the team together ensures that you are getting everyone's expertise and opinions out on the table, and also that everyone understands the positioning and pitch you end up with.

When I work with teams on their positioning, I like to make sure there is representation from sales, marketing, product, and customer success in the room, in addition to the founders/ CEO and anyone else on the executive team who has a strong opinion about how the company wins in the market. It makes sense to have that same team work on the sales pitch as well— at least at a high level. I often have this larger group develop a narrative storyboard to start. Once you agree on the pitch at a storyboard level, a small group, usually consisting of folks from the sales and marketing teams, can work to translate that storyboard into an actual sales pitch with a branded deck, a demo, and a script.

Build a Storyboard First

I often find that teams get hung up on a particular part of a sales pitch while building it. In my opinion, it's much more important that you get the flow of the sales pitch right before dive into the details of the exact words or graphics you need on particular slides. Similarly, I think it's better to determine where the demo should fit and what you want that demo to convey conceptually first. You can worry about the specifics of the demo script later.

In the work I do with clients, when we are working on a sales pitch, I find it helpful to outline the overall structure for the pitch and then fill in the main points under each step as a way of storyboarding out the overall narrative. Once we have that, then we can work on fleshing out the details for each step. Design elements and graphics can be easily added later, once we have a well-fleshed-out storyboard.

Now, let's jump into the starting component of the sales pitch: Insight.

STEP 1
INSIGHT

. . . .

Earlier I talked about sales pitch frameworks used by other companies. One of the things that sets this sales pitch structure apart from those is the way the pitch starts.

Starting with a generic "problem" statement or visible market trend made it difficult for us to differentiate our product from others that claimed to solve the same problem or responded to the same trend. Jumping immediately to a product demo or simply talking about our company left us no room to position ourselves relative to other alternatives in the market. Starting with open questions and discovery didn't give us a structured method to teach buyers a way to think about the market.

You want to start a sales conversation in a way that sets up your differentiated value right from the start. The best way to do that is to start with the market insight that makes your differentiated value important to customers.

I've repeatedly seen how powerful this opening style can be. The fantastic thing about leading with insight is that it:

"A lot of times, people don't know what they want until you show it to them."

STEVE JOBS

1   Immediately establishes your credibility as experienced and knowledgeable about the space.

2   Frames the customer's situation in a way that orients the discussion toward your differentiated value (and nobody else's), right from the beginning.

3   Sets up a discussion with the prospect about the overall market. Starting with market insight makes it easy to transition to talking about the other approaches to solving the problem and space to do discovery.

Your insight is the key element a prospect needs to get to understand the importance of your differentiated value. One way to think about insight is to view it as "the problem inside the problem."

Let's go back to the LevelJump example I used in earlier.

Problems Aren't Unique, Insights Are

LevelJump is in the sales enablement market. Solutions in that market are focused on helping sales teams train salespeople. So how should LevelJump's insight be framed?

The simplest way to define the prospect's problem is, "How do we ensure that salespeople are effectively trained?" But every solution in the market solves that problem, including LevelJump. We can reverse-engineer LevelJump's insight into the market by starting with their differentiated value.

LevelJump is the only sales enablement solution that is built on top of Salesforce. That deeper level of integration allows sales enablement professionals to combine their sales training data with sales performance data. The differentiated value that LevelJump enables for its customers is that it can track the impact of sales training on sales results, giving sales enablement professionals a way to see what's working and what isn't. LevelJump gives the sales enablement team a way to increase revenue through improved sales rep ramp times and to prove the impact of their work. Although other sales enablement solutions can help solve the problem of training sales reps, no other solution can provide a way to measure and improve the impact of that training.

So what is LevelJump's unique insight into the market? What is it that prospects need to know to understand how important their unique value is to them? For prospects to understand LevelJump's unique value, they need to understand that sales enablement is about more than just getting the reps trained and tracking the training. We should be able to measure the success of our sales enablement programs with an improvement of specific sales metrics—for example, the time to first call, time to first deal, and time to reach quota. LevelJump is the only company on the market with this particular insight or point of view on the real underlying problem that needs to be solved with sales enablement.

Your Insight Should Point to Your Value

If done correctly, your insight into the market should direct the conversation toward your value from the onset.

The LevelJump example highlights the deep connection between its unique market point of view and its product's differentiated value—this is critical to establishing a unique position in the market. LevelJump's sales pitch starts by framing the discussion around this insight. How would that play out in a script? Well, since LevelJump usually sells to a head of sales enablement, a first-call discussion with a qualified prospect might start like this:

REP: Hey, thanks for taking the time today. Before we jump into the demo, I wanted to chat a little about how we think about sales enablement. In the companies we have worked with, we've seen that they are investing in sales enablement because it can really make an impact on sales performance and revenue. Every day your reps aren't making quota costs you money. What metrics do you folks use to track enablement?

HEAD OF SALES ENABLEMENT: At the beginning, we were just using a shared drive, and that made it hard to track anything. More recently, we've been looking at using an LMS [learning management system] so we could start tracking which reps have done which training. We've never really thought about how to bring sales metrics into it.

REP: Many of the companies we've worked with have an LMS—it's the perfect tool for corporate training that you need to ensure gets done, like safety or compliance training. For sales training, however, an LMS doesn't give you an easy way to track if your sales enablement programs are improving time to first deal or time to make quota. Folks that run sales enablement often struggle to prove the impact of the programs they are developing. How do you do that for your exec team today?

HEAD OF SALES ENABLEMENT: We really struggle with that, to be honest. I would love a way to show our impact.

How Do You Determine Your Insight?

I believe that every successful company has a unique point of view on the market—they just aren't always great at articulating it. Sometimes you know exactly what your unique insight is because your product was originally designed around it. Other companies develop their insight as they sell more product and gradually gain a better understanding of their customers, their situation, and the value they can bring to the table that other alternative solutions cannot.

In both cases, there may be individual folks on the team who can speak to the company's point of view, but often, sales and marketing teams fall into the trap of focusing on "the problem" or market trends because they're more obvious and therefore easier to identify. The words for these problems and trends already exist in the market, making it easy to write and talk about them.

Luckily, it isn't hard to craft your company's unique insight once you have a method for doing it.

Consider the Point of View of Your Best-Fit Customers

One way of thinking about your unique market insight is to ask this question: "What do your best-fit prospects need to know to understand why your unique value is important to them?"

LevelJump's unique value allows its customers to deliver improved revenue through a better understanding of how their sales enablement is working to drive improved sales metrics. None of the other competitors can deliver that value. So, if you ask what the buyer needs to know to understand LevelJump's unique value, the answer is that they need to think about the

Your unique insight into the market is what leads you to build a product that is different and better than the alternatives.

problem in a different way. They shouldn't be thinking about their problem as "How do I efficiently get sales reps trained?" Any of LevelJump's competitors can solve that problem.

What the buyer should ask is, "How do I improve the sales results for a new rep?" Or, even more specifically, "How do we get a new rep ramped up quicker so they can get a first deal faster and make quota faster?" LevelJump's unique insight into the market is that a company realizes the value of sales onboarding only if it can measure the impact of it with sales metrics.

And that's why LevelJump's sales pitch starts with an implied question: "Why is sales onboarding important?" The answer is that the shorter the sales ramp time, the more revenue the company makes. Starting the narrative here accomplishes everything the company wants in the first step of a pitch:

1   It orients the prospect toward LevelJump's unique value (sales enablement that improves sales results) from the start of the conversation.

2   The insight is unique to LevelJump: none of its competitors look at the market in this way, paving a path for a clearly differentiated narrative.

3   The insight is clear and easy to understand for a prospect that is a good fit for LevelJump (the head of sales enablement at a company that is onboarding a lot of new reps).

Practical Tips

The key to this step is to frame the discussion that comes after it. Sometimes, you will want to follow up your insight with industry research that proves that your insight is true. For example, LevelJump has industry research that shows how much extra revenue a company can generate by speeding up how quickly they ramp up a new sales rep. You will have to decide if you need to present this kind of evidence.

Sometimes, the insight will seem like an obvious statement of fact, and that's okay. In this book, I will give you several examples of sales pitches and you will see that in some cases, the Insight step can seem like a simple statement of fact for a customer. The key is that we are establishing a direction and framing for the discussion in the following step (Alternatives), which is already pointing toward our value. Your insight doesn't need to be complex.

My overall recommendation for this step is that you do not spend too much time on it. In many companies I have worked with, one slide (if you want to use slides) and a minute or two of discussion is more than enough. The goal is to establish that the prospect finds your insight credible and then to move on to the next step as quickly as possible. You never want to skip this step—it's super-important for setting up your differentiated value—but you want to get to the discussion of that value as quickly as you can.

ONCE YOU have framed the discussion around your insight, your next move is to paint a picture of the entire market and the alternative approaches a company may choose to take.

STEP 2
ALTERNATIVES

Many companies avoid talking about competitors because they don't want to be seen as bad-mouthing the competition, which only makes them look bad.

Most companies also feel that no buyer would believe their opinion about a competitor because they are inherently biased. But to make a good choice, buyers need to understand the entire market and the pros and cons of different approaches to solving their problem.

Think of your competition as "approaches to the problem" rather than individual companies. The easiest way for prospects to make sense of a market is to stop thinking about it as an unorganized list of different independent vendors and products and start thinking of it as groups of vendors that share a particular approach to the problem. In a good sales pitch, you are contrasting the different approaches to the problem, rather than trying to compare individual products.

How Should Your Customers Think about Their Options?

The biggest difference between a considered and an unconsidered purchase is that in an unconsidered purchase, buyers don't spend much time, if any, considering their options. But in a considered purchase, they can spend days, or months, figuring out what their options are and how to make a choice. So what's going on in that time frame? The buyer is working through a purchase process to:

- **Clarify the problem.** Why do we need a new solution? What does success look like?

- **Build a list of solution requirements.** What is important for us in a solution? What isn't important? What is possible and what isn't with the current technology on the market?

- **Explore multiple vendors.** Who should be on the shortlist and how do I evaluate these vendors?

This step in the positioning narrative is all about helping customers make sense of their alternatives and the trade-offs associated with each. New start-ups often fall into a common trap of believing that because their solution is new or located in an emerging market space, there is no competition. But there is always an alternative way to accomplish what your solution does, even if that alternative is manual processes and Excel spreadsheets. The key here is to understand what a customer sees as an alternative to your solution, not what you would necessarily consider a direct competitor.

Position Yourself against the Fearsome Status Quo

When you sell to businesses, you are often competing with solutions that companies adopted because they were free and well known, and because they did a good enough job for the time being. From a customer's perspective, these are alternative ways of doing the same job your software does, even if you would never describe these solutions as your competition.

For example, Excel is the most common alternative for tech companies selling to businesses. I've seen Excel used as a CRM, an invoice tracker, a customer support solution, a financial modeler, and a business intelligence tool. Doing things manually is also a perfectly viable option for many tasks. And many companies will use a "monolith" software package (their accounting, ERP, CRM, or e-commerce system) to do tasks that are on the periphery of what these solutions were originally built to do.

Sales teams in software companies tend to describe losing to a status quo solution as losing to "no decision," but that's dangerous thinking for sales and marketing teams. A decision *was* made, whether it was to stick with what they were doing longer term or, as happens more often, to delay making a decision altogether.

You need to view the customer's option to stick with the status quo as a competitive alternative, even if you don't view the solution they are using as direct competition.

**Consider Direct Competitors,
but Only if They Land on a Prospect's Shortlist**

Besides the status quo alternative, you also need to understand what other solutions are landing on a buyer's shortlist. Most business buyers don't simply select the first solution they come across. They do their homework and narrow down a shortlist of alternatives to examine more closely. Just as you need to look at the status quo the way a customer does, you also need to look at shortlist competitors from the customer's point of view.

At this step of the sales pitch, you will need to stay rooted in the facts of the market as it exists today and in the near future. Although your product and strategy teams might be tracking dozens of potential "horizon" competitors (competitors you may have in the future), you don't need to position against anything a customer does not currently consider. There is also a real danger associated with giving prospects new approaches to think about. They might feel they need to go back and research these newly introduced options, further delaying a purchase decision. Companies that orient their marketing and sales stories too closely around a future vision of the market are only giving buyers more reasons to do what they are most inclined to do—delay making any purchase at all.

Positioning and the sales pitch that it represents will evolve over time. When, and if, a competitor starts showing up on prospect shortlists, you will go back to your positioning and determine if it and your sales pitch will need an adjustment.

Group Competitors into "Approaches"

Your goal at this step in the sales pitch is to help the buyer make sense of their options. To do that, you need to group all the alternatives in the market into different "approaches" to solving the problem. The easiest way to make sense of a market is to think of it as groups of vendors that share a particular approach to the job they satisfy.

For example, you might have a set of status quo alternatives, such as using an intern in combination with a spreadsheet or

We don't compete
with companies or
products. We compete
with approaches.

using Microsoft Word and manual processes done by a junior employee. These could be grouped together as "manual labor plus a spreadsheet." The grouping should be seen as a way of helping your customers understand the important facets of how those companies have approached the problem.

Grouping Competitors Helps Your Customers Understand Your Value

Suppose you sell a project management tool specifically designed for agencies that build custom software products. Your ideal customer is an agency with fewer than thirty people that works on multiple projects simultaneously. The product's key points of value are that it is easy to use and manage, and has specific features for agencies. The most important feature is that the product allows visibility into employee use so you can smartly assign work tasks across multiple projects.

Your company's insight is that for agencies that do custom development, margins are incredibly thin. That means optimizing their resources can make the difference between life and death for these businesses.

Your competitive alternatives might be broken up into "manual solutions" such as spreadsheets and Word documents or other ways of manually tracking who is working on what; "easy to use, all-purpose project management tools" like Trello or Basecamp; and "enterprise project management tools" such as Jira or Atlassian.

Breaking up the market in this way highlights that there are tools more suitable to smaller businesses and some more suitable for larger businesses. In dividing it up this way, we are helping best-fit buyers (multi-project agencies of fewer than thirty employees) understand that an "all-purpose tool" might be lacking features they might specifically require, but similarly, an "enterprise tool" would be too complex and expensive for a company of their size. This sets up a conversation with a prospect in which you can easily highlight the gap you fill in the market.

Should You Call Out Competitors by Name?

This is your decision to make, but I generally prefer not to name competitors unless we are almost guaranteed that the prospect has already looked at them as a potential solution. We don't want to give buyers a reason to go away and research a new set of competitors. As part of the discovery the rep is doing during this step in the sales pitch, they can easily ask the prospect what other solutions they are considering, and then categorize them. That said, if there is a competitor that is seen in nearly every deal, I wouldn't hesitate to explicitly name the elephant in the room.

It's Okay to Position a Competitor in a Way They Would Disagree with as Long as You Believe That It's Objectively True

When you group these competitors, it's important to do so according to your point of view on how they should be categorized. This may not be the way the competitors categorize themselves, and it may also conflict with how some industry analysts or other third parties categorize them. Often, competitors are exaggerating their capabilities in certain ways or marketing them in a way that is misleading for customers (either deliberately or not).

This is your opportunity to educate your prospects about where you believe your competitors really land in the market

Discovery is
a conversation,
not a lecture.

after you strip away all the marketing buzzwords and subterfuge. However, this *does not* give you a license to lie. At this step, it is critical to present your case as objectively as possible. Your role is to be an informed guide—one who has the customer's best interests at heart. Nothing will destroy a customer's trust in your advice faster than catching you out in a lie.

Outline the Pros and Cons of Each Alternative for Different Customers

Once you have categorized the alternative approaches, you need to outline the pros and cons of each alternative for different types of customers. For our project management tool example, that might look something like this:

APPROACH	PROS	CONS
Manual solutions	Free and easy to get started	Very difficult to manage resources across projects
Easy to use, all-purpose project management tools	Low cost, easy to use	Lack multi-project resource planning tools, difficult to track across a large number of projects
Enterprise project management tools	Very full featured, track resources across multiple projects	Expensive, difficult to deploy and use

At this point, you have painted a picture of the entire market for the prospect. You can now have a clear conversation with the customer about the different approaches available to them and why they may or may not want to take each approach.

The pros and cons of each alternative approach can be crafted with a qualified prospect in mind. You generally already know something about the customer's current situation because they have already been qualified. Since the key value proposition is around planning resourcing across multiple projects, prospects who don't need that would already be disqualified. Similarly, larger companies that might want an "enterprise" solution would also be disqualified.

This Is a Discovery Conversation, Not a Lecture

The Alternatives step is where you want to do discovery with the client. This discovery should happen in the form of a conversation with the prospect rather than a lecture from the sales rep.

A common mistake inexperienced sellers make in discovery is asking questions about the customer's pain and problems with the expectation that prospects already know exactly what they are looking for. As I've said earlier, many buyers have never purchased a product like yours before. Often, they are not entirely sure what their purchase criteria are or should be, and they are still learning what is and isn't possible with the current solutions on the market. They understand their immediate problem, but there may be dimensions to the problem they haven't thought about yet. A salesperson quizzing a buyer on what exactly they're looking for might, at best, result in the buyer giving some fuzzy answers to try to move the discussion along. At worst, this kind of questioning could leave the buyer feeling annoyed and worried that the sales rep doesn't know any more about the market than they do.

Instead, you want to use this step in the narrative to have a back-and-forth discovery conversation in which you are learning about the customer's situation, but you are also teaching the customer about the market. For example, the conversation could potentially go like this:

REP: We work with customer software development shops like yours that are looking for a new way to manage projects and resources across projects. Often, we see companies like yours picking one of these three categories of solutions. I understand you folks have been tracking your projects manually. How's that working out for you?

PROSPECT: We designed a set of templates in Excel and have been tracking projects like that since we started the business. Lately, we have seen some growth and it's become a bit more complex to get a handle on who is working on what.

REP: We hear this a lot. Most of the companies that have adopted our tool have outgrown manual solutions. The project management space is really crowded, but we find most tools can be described as either easy-to-use all-purpose project management or more enterprise-oriented tools, like Jira. Have you folks looked at any other solutions so far?

PROSPECT: Well, Jira would be overkill for us. We have looked at Trello and we love the simplicity of what they do.

REP: Trello is a great product and certainly easy to use. Have you looked at the resource planning capabilities of Trello? We have found that most tools like Trello weren't designed with agencies in mind. They typically don't support views and analysis that cross multiple projects, something that is critical to the agency customers that we work with.

PROSPECT: We haven't seen much in their tool that would help us with that, so, yes, that does appear to be a gap.

This step in the sales pitch should really be a dialogue with the customer. Combined with actively teaching the prospect the pros and cons of other alternatives, it will include discovery questions such as: How are you handling this today? How is that approach working for you? What other solutions are you looking at?

Practical Tips

People often ask me how the Alternatives step should look if they are using slides. Should this be illustrated with a picture? A table? Something else? I have seen companies do this step in several different ways. Some use a table like the one I used above. Some draw a picture with the different alternatives mapped onto a four-by-four grid. I have also seen many companies do this step without a slide at all; they simply have a lightly scripted conversation. Personally, I like a table, but I keep the number of words to a minimum so that it is more of a conversation guide than something a rep might be tempted to read.

As with the previous step, I also would caution you to be careful not to spend too much time here. It's critical to have the conversation, but the goal here is to paint a picture of the market for the prospect, help them understand the pros and cons of the different approaches while simultaneously getting your discovery questions answered, and then move on.

ONCE YOU have discussed the trade-offs associated with your alternatives, it's time to move on to "The Perfect World." In this step, you will make sure the prospect is aligned with your point of view on the characteristics of a perfect solution for a buyer like them.

STEP 3
THE PERFECT WORLD

· · · · · · · · · · · · ·

The purpose of this step in the sales pitch is to clearly state what you believe the purchase criteria should be for a solution, assuming the buyer is a best-fit customer and they agree with your point of view.

The is the last step in "the setup" phase of the sales pitch. You can think of this step as the conclusion to the discussion you just had about the alternative solutions a prospect might choose. That conversation would have highlighted the advantages and downsides of each solution. In this step, you imagine a "perfect solution" for the type of customer you serve, based on the conclusions you can draw from the previous discussion. That perfect solution would provide prospects with the important upsides of each alternative while avoiding the major drawbacks. If you have done this well, the list of characteristics of the perfect solution will map to your differentiated value.

Getting Aligned on Your Point of View on the Market

The goal of this step is to ensure the prospect understands and agrees with your point of view on what is and isn't important for a buyer like them. You do this by reiterating the insight you shared in Step 1 and the conclusions you can draw from the pros and cons of the alternative solutions you discussed in Step 2. If you continue with the example from the previous chapter, the conversation at this step would go something like this:

REP: We know that effective resource planning is incredibly important for agencies. In a perfect world, you would have a project management tool that

- is as easy to use as a low-end, all-purpose tool like Trello,

- but is designed to help you manage a growing team across a growing number of projects,

- all without the cost or complexity of traditional enterprise project management tools.

Right?

That "right?" from the sales rep is a critical turning point in this pitch. It goes one of two ways now: 1) The customer doesn't agree, which generally means they have disqualified themselves. If they don't see your point of view as critically important to them, then your unique value simply isn't going to resonate, and essentially you have nothing to sell them. Or, 2) the customer responds with, "Yep, you're right," and you have already done the hard work of making the sale.

The customer has agreed that their purchase criteria should look like the above list. They have chosen the value only you can deliver. Now all that is left to do is show them how your solution delivers it. Most importantly, if the prospect agrees with you at this point, they have also agreed that the alternatives can't meet their needs. The deal is yours to lose from this point forward.

Practical Tips
. . . .

In this step, you are making sure the prospect agrees with your point of view on the world. If it is clear the customer is with you, then there is no need to linger here. Simply move on to the next step. Overall, reps should move through the first three steps of the sales pitch—Insight, Alternatives, and The Perfect World—fairly quickly. For many companies I have worked with, the setup part of a first call is done in around five to ten minutes, or less if the first call is scheduled for less than an hour. A great setup is setting the context for your differentiated value. If you are taking too long to get to the value step, you risk losing the customer's interest before you have arrived at the meat of the pitch.

FROM THIS point forward, you will switch from talking about the market context to talking about your company and the solution you can deliver. You have established what the important criteria are for a solution; now, your job is to show how your solution stacks up against these criteria. You are now passing from "the setup" phase of the sales pitch to "the follow-through."

A SALES PITCH STORY: POSTMAN

POSTMAN STARTED as a side project to solve a specific problem: Abhinav Asthana, Postman's CEO and co-founder, set out to create a tool that would simplify the testing process for APIs (application programming interfaces, which allow developers to interact with computer applications). As Postman expanded, so did the platform's functionality, which today includes tools to help developers across the lifecycle of API development from design, testing, and documentation to sharing APIs. In 2022, Postman had twenty million users globally. Half a million companies use Postman, and they have the largest API hub in the world.

Postman needed a sales narrative to help IT executives understand the value it delivers. Buyers were accustomed to using separate tools for different stages in the API lifecycle and were confused about which of these tools Postman might replace and which it would integrate with. What Postman is really selling is a new way to think about APIs and the potential value they can deliver to companies. Their narrative needs to answer the key question, "Why use Postman instead of the way we build APIs today?"

April says: The pitch starts with Postman's market insight.

APIs are becoming a crucial building block for software development. Increasingly, APIs are a critical way through which applications interact with each other. Low-quality, difficult-to-consume APIs are putting both customer experience and revenue at risk. Companies must quickly deliver high-quality APIs that are easily consumable.

> **April says:** Next, Postman needs to help buyers understand the current landscape of tools (alternatives) and where they fit.

Companies today are developing APIs as an afterthought instead of treating them as a driver of business value. APIs are built, managed, and distributed using a mix of siloed tools for designing, testing, documenting, and distributing them, each used by separate teams across the API lifecycle. While each tool does the job it was meant to do, working in siloes leads to a set of serious drawbacks:

- It is very difficult to govern the quality of the end-to-end API development process.

- APIs are often badly designed, inconsistent, and poorly documented.

- APIs are ultimately difficult for consumers to use and understand.

> **April says:** Now we can define the characteristics of a "perfect" solution.

If we believe in the importance of APIs to our business, we need to take an "API-first" approach. That approach would:

- Provide an integrated set of tools spanning the API lifecycle to improve quality.

- Make it easy for teams to collaborate to efficiently solve problems and speed time to market.

- Provide a repository containing APIs and the documentation, test cases, and everything else consumers need all in one place, making APIs easy to consume and use.

April says: Now we can move on to the meat of the pitch—in this case, a conversation and structured demo that shows how Postman delivers the value described in the perfect solution step.

Postman is an API development platform for building and using APIs.

Postman simplifies each step of the API lifecycle and streamlines collaboration so you can create better APIs—faster.

The Value Postman Delivers

Improves API quality using an integrated set of tools spanning the entire API lifecycle: In a sales pitch, Postman can show the range of tools across design, testing, development, and distribution, all delivered in a single integrated platform.

Workspaces make it easy for developers to collaborate to solve problems efficiently and speed time to market: Here, the rep can demo Postman's Workspaces feature.

Improves customer adoption by making APIs easier to consume: Lastly, a demo could show the API repository.

> **April says:** The pitch then winds up with a case study as proof that Postman can deliver the value points covered in the demo, and then it ends by getting an agreement with the prospect to move forward to the next stage of their sales process.

About Postman, Asthana told me, "The narrative we created around 'an API-first world' really helped customers understand our way of looking at the business potential for APIs and let us carve out a unique space in the market."

STEP 4
THE INTRODUCTION

· ·

Now you are ready to switch your focus from the market to your solution. The first step is to introduce the company and the solution.

If you are a multi-product company, this is your chance to position your entire company, the products you offer, and the particular product that this pitch is focused on (assuming there is only one product that is the focus of this pitch). If you are a single-product company, then this is a simple introduction to the product.

The structure of your introduction in the pitch will depend on your specific sales strategy. For single-product start-ups, this step is an introduction to the product at a high level. Often, this can be done by introducing the market category and briefly outlining what your product is designed to do. Multi-product companies will often introduce everything the company can do and explain how this particular product fits in their portfolio.

In this introduction, a diagram is a common tool that either illustrates the component pieces of your solution or shows how your solution might fit into the prospect's existing technology stack. There are three common diagrams I see used at this step: the family diagram, the platform diagram, and the "marketecture" diagram. (You can find these and other reference materials at **aprildunford.com/books**.)

The family diagram: For multi-product companies, the product family diagram is a clear and easy way to describe all the products in the family and how they fit together.

The platform diagram: For companies that sell a platform, a diagram can be a concise way to show prospects the range of functionality that is included as part of the platform. Components might be available separately or they might be included. Sometimes, you will want to expose packaging options in the diagram. For example, if there are add-on components that customers don't want and worry they will be forced to pay for, it could make sense in the diagram to explicitly signal that these components are entirely optional. Other times, you may want to show the full spectrum of functionality and leave the packaging and pricing discussions for later. For example, if the ideal combination of options is dependent on understanding a customer's needs first, you would want to expose everything in the diagram and leave the discussion of the precise configuration until later in the sales process.

The "marketecture" diagram: For certain types of products, particularly those with technical buyers or infrastructure products (such as data, security, monitoring, and networking), it's often important to illustrate how your solutions fit in with everything else the buyer already has. Unlike a technical and detailed architecture diagram, a "marketecture" diagram gives buyers enough information to understand the

"Proactive guidance
has a demonstrably
positive effect on
win rates."

MATTHEW DIXON & BRENT ADAMSON

major components of the system and how those components interface or interact with each other. The marketecture diagram should be easy for a sales rep to explain and a buyer to understand. Done well, a good marketecture diagram clearly shows which solutions your product interacts with and which it may replace.

Practical Tips

Orient the prospect quickly around what you are and what you do, but then move on. The next step dives deeper into the value you deliver, and you will want to spend the bulk of your time on this step in the sales pitch.

STEP 5
DIFFERENTIATED VALUE

. . . .

Helping customers understand the value only you can deliver should be the centerpiece of everything you do in marketing and sales. Value is why customers buy your product.

Customers don't care about your features or capabilities, but they do care about what those features can do for their business. And that's why the Differentiated Value step should be where you spend the most time in a first sales call.

In this step, you will clearly describe the value only you can deliver and dive into the features that enable that value. Earlier, I talked about how the components of positioning are the crucial inputs to the sales pitch. None of those components is more important than differentiated value. Much of what you discussed with the prospect in the setup phase of the pitch (the insight, the alternatives, the perfect solution) gives your prospect context on how the value you can deliver differs from other approaches, and why that value matters a lot to a particular type of customer.

If you have done your job well in previous steps, you have already helped the buyer understand why this value is important. Now, your main goal is to demonstrate *how* you deliver that value to your prospect.

Many companies choose to do this step using a scripted demo with slides. Some use a demo only and others will only use slides. I've seen companies do an excellent job at this step in each of those ways. But when you are working through how you want to do this step, there are some key points you'll need to consider.

Demo and Slides

Many companies I have worked with start the Differentiated Value step with a slide that introduces the value themes. Then they move to a detailed demo that walks through the key features that support each theme, and then move back to the slide to reiterate the themes before moving to the next step.

I like this approach because it helps you focus on the value themes and remember them as key takeaways. If you choose to go this route, I encourage you to keep the text on the slides to a minimum and resist the urge to list every feature. Remember, the point of the Differentiated Value step is to demonstrate how your features deliver the value. But the most important thing you want the prospect to remember at the end of the step is the value—not the features.

If one or more of your value themes don't lend themselves to a demo, using a mix of slides and a demo works for this step. Value themes related to support/services, pricing models, or packaging would fall into this category. You can work those into the script or cover them in a slide.

Demo Only

In many cases, the best way to describe how a product does a particular thing is to show how it works. For example, if you have a value theme related to the user experience of your product, your reps could attempt to describe it, but it will be more impactful to show it in action. The way the demo is organized is key.

This is *not* a product walkthrough. You should not be highlighting every feature of the product. The goal is to reinforce your differentiated value by showing how the product delivers that. If you have three distinct value themes, the demo should be organized around them. The script for the demo should be organized along these lines:

- We deliver a combination of Value A, Value B, and Value C for our customers.

- Let's start with Value A: here are the features that deliver that.

- Now let's move to Value B: here are the features that deliver that.

- Lastly, we have Value C: here's how we do that.

The key here is that the demo is organized to reinforce your differentiated value and make that real for prospects by showing them how you deliver it.

A great product demo puts features in the context of the value they enable.

Slides Only

It's not unusual, especially for complex enterprise software, to have a first call that does *not* include a demo. For products like a data warehouse, cloud infrastructure software, and security software, often there isn't much to demonstrate. And even if you did a demo, it wouldn't mean much if it was not highly customized. You have a few choices in this situation.

Sometimes, it makes sense to create an example of what a customer implementation might look like and use that in parts of the Differentiated Value step to illustrate particular capabilities. Be sure to highlight what is and isn't included in your product. I've seen companies get in trouble at this stage because the customer gets the impression that these customizations are included in the base product.

Although you might want to do a customized demo as part of your sales process, it's unlikely it would happen on a first call, as the prospect has been qualified but you haven't done a deeper discovery with them yet. In this case, the custom demo would be the next step in the sales process (and asking to book a meeting to show the custom demo would be incorporated in the last step of the pitch, The Ask. More on this later).

Practical Tips

One of the most common mistakes I see start-ups make at this step is including capabilities that are important to customers but don't exactly deliver value. For example, it's possible you sell to financial services and your customers will not be able to buy your product unless it meets their security requirements. In a typical sales conversation, this might come up as objections by the prospect that sound like deal-breakers. For example, the prospect might say: "We can't buy your software if it doesn't meet our security compliance requirements," or, "We can't buy your software if it doesn't play nicely with our existing ERP system."

Often, capabilities like these aren't differentiating because any vendor wishing to sell to this category of customers would have to meet this functionality requirement. But even though your product is SOC 2 certified, which is important for a customer to know, it's not a differentiated value. Still, you don't want the customer to exclude you from the running because they assume you don't have that capability.

In this sales pitch structure, these kinds of capabilities are best addressed in the objection-handling step. I'll talk more about that in Step 7.

IN THIS STEP, you have learned how to incorporate the value only your solution can provide and the features that support that value. However, you should never expect that your prospects will take your claims at face value. This is why you move into the Proof step of the pitch.

A SALES PITCH STORY: FUNNEL

FUNNEL WAS founded by Fredrik Skantze and Per Made, who envisioned an easier way for digital marketers to analyze their online marketing performance. They observed that digital marketers were spending an increasing amount of time and effort gathering and making sense of their data across marketing channels. Funnel set out to make this faster and easier by creating a solution that pulls data from any marketing source, prepares it to be analyzed, then makes it available to any tool the business needs to use to analyze the data so it can be understood. In other words, Funnel makes it easy for marketers to deeply understand their data to improve their results.

The landscape of alternative approaches to Funnel is complex. Some marketing teams use connectors to pull data from individual channels into a spreadsheet to be analyzed. Other teams adopt an "IT-centric" approach where connectors pull the data and then it is transformed and stored in a data warehouse. IT gives marketing access to a data snapshot that they can analyze using business intelligence tools. Lastly, some teams use a marketing analytics platform that gives them data visualization combined with basic functionality spanning connectors, transformation, and analysis.

Funnel is sometimes compared to products with only a fraction of its capabilities. At its core, Funnel is a marketing data hub. In order to sell prospects on the value of a data hub, the prospects first need to understand how that approach is different from what they currently do.

April says: The pitch starts with Funnel's market insight. The key to recognizing Funnel's value is understanding that data is critical to a marketing team's success, yet teams struggle to collect and use their data.

Great digital marketing is all about data. We depend on deeply understanding marketing data to optimize our digital marketing spend. But gathering data across channels, normalizing it, and producing metrics the business needs to analyze and improve performance is difficult, time-consuming, and error-prone.

April says: Next, Funnel needs to map the alternatives and illustrate the gaps.

Connectors and spreadsheets: These are simple to get started with but leave you with siloed data that isn't normalized across channels. Mapping fields across channels is hard. Changes break the spreadsheet, making your historical data useless.

The "IT stack" data solution: This lets your IT team use the data for other purposes, but marketing is left with a static snapshot of data they can't control and, therefore, can't trust. New requirements or changes need to go through your already overwhelmed IT department, limiting marketing's ability to move quickly.

Marketing analytics platforms: These give some basic capabilities across dashboarding, connectors, and transformation, with a focus on using the platform for everything as opposed to being able to use best-of-breed tools (i.e., for reporting or analytics). These platforms often require technical expertise to stand up and maintain. Marketers again become dependent on the vendor or their IT team, hampering their ability to move quickly.

> **April says:** Now Funnel can define the characteristics of a "perfect" solution—in this case, they are defining a marketing data hub and the value companies could get from having one.

If we believe that marketing's success relies on our ability to analyze data, we will conclude that marketing needs a central data hub. One that:

- Easily pulls accurate data from any source

- Stores all the data in a central place that marketing owns and can trust (that the data is accurate and up to date)

- Prepares the data for analysis automatically

- Makes it easy to share data to analyze it any way marketing needs to—with spreadsheets, data warehouses, reporting and analytics tools, etc.

> **April says:** Next is the meat of the pitch, Funnel's value.

Funnel is a marketing hub for data designed to help marketing teams get control over their data to improve performance. The value Funnel delivers:

- **Brings all marketing data together from any source.** The rep can demo how, in a few clicks, Funnel can connect to data from any source without code.

- **Stores data in a central hub, giving marketing teams control over the data they need to improve digital marketing performance.** The rep can show the data hub, including the raw data, transformed data, and data logic.

- **Automatically makes siloed raw data business-ready.** The rep can show how automatic mapping works and how users can control how data is mapped without code.

- **Easily makes marketing data available wherever it is needed.** The rep can demonstrate connecting a business intelligence (BI) tool to Funnel in a few clicks.

April says: The pitch then winds up with a case study as proof that Funnel can deliver the value points covered in the value section, and then ends by getting an agreement with the prospect to move forward to the next stage of their sales process.

STEP 6
PROOF

. . . .

Since the dawn of mass marketing, vendors have been spinning, stretching, and just plain ignoring the truth.

Buyers have learned that just because the company says it can do something does not make it so. So, if you are going to make a claim of value, you will need to back it up with some proof.

Proof can take many different forms. When I am working with start-ups on their sales pitches, they often assume that "proof" must be empirical, or something to which they can assign concrete numbers. Claims like "30 percent faster," or "save 10 hours per week on administration tasks," or "99 percent uptime" are examples of empirical proof that you may have validated either across a large group of customers or with a third party. These are great proof points, and if you have them, you should consider using them at this step.

However, not all claims lend themselves to this type of proof. Sometimes value is difficult to measure. For example, suppose one of your core value points is that you make it easy for a user to get up and running on the software. You could show that directly in a demo, and that would help the buyer get a feel for how easy it might be. You might be able to get data that shows that users on your system feel fully trained in a day versus a week for your competitors. You can also prove value by having customers talk about their own experiences and how easy it was for them to get their users up and running on the system. Remember that you saying something about your own product isn't proof, but a customer saying it is.

Here is a list of some ways you can prove that a value point is true:

1 Customer case studies

2 Third-party verification

3 Certification—for example, you have SOC 2 compliance for security

4 Statistics that are validated by your customers

5 Customer quotes

6 Quotes or reviews from industry analysts

7 Industry research or survey results from third parties

8 Awards

Practical Tips

This section of the sales pitch should reflect the situation of the prospect as closely as possible. For example, you may have a product that serves a wide variety of customers, from banks to manufacturing plants. If you use case studies as proof at this step, ideally you would show a banking case study to a bank and a manufacturing case study to a manufacturer. Similarly,

"Facts tell, but stories sell."

BRYAN EISENBERG

if you are showing quotes or reviews of your product, the person you are quoting should be as similar as possible (in terms of role at the company and their seniority) to the prospect you are talking to.

Sometimes it is natural to include proof points at the same time as you are talking about the value points themselves. If so, I think that's a good way to do it. This step doesn't necessarily need to give proof for every value point if you have presented some proof for those value points earlier in the sales pitch.

IT IS NORMAL for a customer to have questions during a sales pitch. The next step is an optional one for handling important objections that you don't want to leave unanswered, regardless of whether or not a customer raised them during the pitch.

STEP 7
OBJECTIONS

· ·

A good salesperson will handle any questions or objections a customer may have as they occur in the sales meeting. However, you may notice that there are common objections that are crucial to address in the first meeting, whether or not the customer has raised them.

This step is optional. If you find there are common unspoken objections you need to handle, this is when you would do that, but if not, you can skip this step.

Imagine your customer has arrived at this step in the meeting and likes what you say. They agree with your view of the market, are excited by the value you could bring to their company, and believe you can do what you say you can—but they are still skeptical. I recommend you simply address the specific concerns head-on, even if the prospect hasn't raised them.

Typical objections and responses might sound something like this:

PROSPECT: This sounds difficult to deploy.

REP: We have a dedicated team that will help you with deployment. Here's what a typical deployment schedule looks like, and it usually it takes two weeks.

• • •

PROSPECT: The price is likely too high for us. / We aren't sure we have the budget.

REP: This is the way our pricing model works and what this would look like for three different types of customers. We can give you a specific quote for your situation whenever you are ready.

• • •

PROSPECT: Getting end users to adopt this will be difficult.

REP: We have a dedicated training team that will work with you to get users onboarded. Here's what some of our customers have to say about user onboarding.

• • •

PROSPECT: We don't want everything now, just pieces of it.

REP: Our platform is modular, and it isn't uncommon that customers want to start small and grow with us. Here's how those steps usually look over time.

• • •

PROSPECT: Anything we adopt needs to be compliant with certain regulations. / Anything we adopt needs to integrate with our existing infrastructure.

REP: We are currently compliant with all regulations necessary for a solution like this, and we would be happy to walk your technical team through this. We integrate easily with your current infrastructure through our well-documented API. Most deployments take about two weeks for integration work. Our services team can help plan how best to do that, and we would be happy to talk to your technical team about how that would work.

Helping Customers Understand How to Move Forward
....

For many of the companies I have worked with, this step is when they address potential objections in regard to deployment or change management. These are good issues to handle at this step because they lead naturally into the next section, which is where you will talk about what you think the best next step would be for the prospect.

As we learned earlier in this book, clients are fearful of change and will often stick with their status quo solution, even when they dislike it. This step is a great place to begin alleviating the prospect's fear of change or failure. The most common unspoken objection we have in B2B technology sales is a fear that the deployment will be difficult or runs the risk of failing altogether. Most companies will try to help smooth the transition to their software through professional services help, training, onboarding assistance, hands-on technical support, and more.

At this step, it's also good to get specific on what the timelines look like for a deployment because prospects will often

Anticipating and handling unspoken objections is often a critical component of a first sales call.

overestimate how long and difficult this phase will be. Here are some examples:

REP: We know that switching providers for a solution like this is never easy, so we make it as seamless as possible to get started with us. Our clients often start with a small initial deployment. Our team can help you define what the requirements would be, and usually we can get a client like you up and running in as little as a week.

. . .

REP: Most of our clients find it helpful to start with a proof of concept, where you can get a feel for how our solution works with your data. We can easily migrate the data into our system for you in as little as a day, and we don't need the assistance of your IT department.

. . .

REP: Some clients worry about how our system would work with your existing tools. We have a set of pre-built integrations that cover most tools teams like yours use. We also have an API that allows for custom integrations.

. . .

REP: We know that you operate in a regulated industry, so our solution is SOC 2 and ISO 27001 certified. We have worked with X, Y, and Z corporations and satisfied their compliance and security requirements, so we are sure we can satisfy yours. We often find it helpful to meet directly with the IT team at some point to help them understand the depth of our security posture.

Practical Tips

Remember that this step is optional. I've seen products for which there simply aren't any common unspoken objections, because either the prospects have raised their concerns during the setup phase of the sales pitch or the objections are handled as part of the rep's explanation of the differentiated value. If there aren't any objections to handle, you can simply skip this step entirely.

What about a common objection that you don't have a good response for? In this case, I would not recommend that you deliberately call the objection out if the customer hasn't raised it. That said, if in the course of building this sales pitch you realize there is an objection you simply aren't doing a great job of handling, take this as a sign that fixing the problem should move up in your list of priorities.

NOW YOU are ready to move the pitch smoothly into the final step, The Ask, a discussion of who would need to be involved, and what you would need to do to get agreement to move forward with that.

STEP 8
THE ASK

· · · · · · · · · · · · · · · ·

Just like the other stages of the sales pitch, you want to be deliberate about the way your conversation comes to an end. That includes helping your prospect decide what to do next.

It isn't unusual to see inexperienced sales folks get to the end of a sales meeting and leave it up to the prospect entirely to decide what the next step should be. Now is the time to embrace your role as a guide helping the buyer through the purchase process.

"The Ask" will depend on what you believe is the best next step in your purchase process. For example, if your best-fit customers usually run a proof of concept (POC) and your team wants to encourage that, suggesting how to move forward with a POC would be a good ask, using these questions as guidelines:

- Who needs to be involved with a POC?

- Do we need to set up an additional meeting with those folks?

- Are there other steps that need to be taken (signed non-disclosure agreements, a completed security review, etc.)?
- If so, how would we get them completed?

The next step could be a fully customized demo in front of a wider group of stakeholders, getting the client signed up for a trial version of the product, asking if you can prepare a detailed quote, or simply asking for the sale. Whatever it is, be sure that the meeting doesn't end without a clear next step.

Sometimes the Next Step Is for the Customer to Look Elsewhere

Not every buyer should or will move past a first sales call. The goal in the first call should not be to get every customer closer to making a purchase. Instead, your goal is to get every *good-fit* buyer past this stage. A good first sales call will get good-fit prospects excited to move forward; it should also make clear to bad-fit prospects that this is not the solution for them. Ideally, your qualification step will weed out most of the bad-fit clients, but don't expect it to weed them all out. Quickly getting misaligned prospects out of your sales process is good for everyone. It's good for buyers, who don't want to waste their time, and for sales teams who can concentrate their efforts on prospects that are less likely to chew up resources and then drop out of the sales process later.

Practical Tips

. . . .

Mature sales organizations will have a documented and tested sales process with a set of distinct steps they move though before a deal is closed. Many start-ups fail to have an ask at the end of their sales pitch at all ("Call us if you have any questions!" doesn't count). If your company is new and your sales process is less evolved, a good starting point to get some structure is to be consistent in what you ask the customer to do after the first sales call. This will also give you a starting point to at least test which call to action works best with your customer set.

YOU HAVE now completed the storyboard for your sales pitch. You know how to set up your pitch with customer insight, how to help customers understand the market while you get a better understanding of their situation, how to structure a value-oriented demo with proof, how to explicitly handle unspoken objections, and how to ask for the next step. Your next task now is to construct a deck, demo, and script that reflect this storyline and then test it to ensure it resonates with your prospects.

A SALES PITCH STORY: GEARSET

GEARSET'S FOUNDERS, Kevin Boyle and Matt Dickens, met at Redgate Software, a company selling a Database DevOps solution. When Redgate adopted Salesforce as a CRM, Boyle and Dickens got front-row seats to the process of customizing the solution and releasing it to the team. They noticed that the tools and processes they were accustomed to using to release software quickly and reliably (what we would describe as DevOps) didn't exist on Salesforce, which left them with a manual and error-prone process. This seemed like an opportunity for a couple of developers working in the world of DevOps. In 2017, they formed Gearset, today the world's leading Salesforce DevOps solution.

As Gearset grew, there were both new and incumbent competitors that, on the surface, seemed identical to Gearset. They claimed to deliver the same value, seemed to mirror Gearset's messaging, and declared "leadership" in the market while having a much smaller customer base than Gearset has. Gearset's sales pitch challenge is to help prospects understand what Gearset can do differently and why that matters.

Gearset's Differentiators

Gearset's main differentiators come from their background in DevOps. First, they believe teams deploying Salesforce releases should work like any other development team, using standard DevOps tool sets and processes as far as possible. In contrast, Gearset's rivals chose to implement their own solutions for things like project management and source control.

Second, Gearset is built outside of Salesforce, allowing the team to leverage the most suitable technologies to provide tailored solutions to problems unique to Salesforce, like sophisticated comparison, merging, and deployment for Salesforce metadata. Gearset's rivals chose to build on top of Salesforce, constraining them within its UX paradigms, and to focus on breadth over depth.

And third, Gearset has a much larger customer set than any of their competitors, making them a deeply experienced, trusted choice.

The Gearset Pitch

Because the competitive landscape for Gearset is limited, they can compress the sales pitch structure by not explicitly listing the pros and cons of multiple alternative approaches.

April says: The conversation starts with their key insight, which is that the same factors that lead to the benefits of a DevOps approach for software releases in general also apply to Salesforce releases.

DevOps is now mainstream, as software teams understand the improvements they can get in the speed and stability of their releases and helping teams collaborate. We are starting to see the same benefits when adopting DevOps for Salesforce. But we know that not all DevOps transformations are equally effective. The same factors that lead to a successful DevOps transformation in other software teams apply when adopting Salesforce DevOps.

April says: At this point, we have already set up Gearset's main differentiated value—maximizing Salesforce DevOps success by leveraging best-in-class DevOps tools, processes, and expertise. We can therefore move straight to the definition of a perfect solution.

What Are the Key Factors That Lead to DevOps Success?

1 Standard tools and processes: we would expect any Salesforce DevOps solution to take full advantage of the existing standard tools for source control and project management.

2 A partner with deep expertise and experience in DevOps in general, and DevOps for Salesforce in particular.

3 A broad set of capabilities specifically tailored to the hardest Salesforce challenges around release management.

April says: Now we can move on to the meat of the pitch: the value that only Gearset delivers. In this pitch, they will want to be very specific about certain claims—for example, the number of customers—to combat competitors attempting to make similar claims.

Gearset is the industry's most trusted Salesforce DevOps platform. They are a team of DevOps experts working to make Salesforce teams more effective.

The value that Gearset delivers:

1 **DevOps the right way. Gearset fully embraces the standard enterprise DevOps tool set, giving Salesforce teams the full benefit of DevOps.** The rep would explain and demo how Gearset supports GitHub, Jira, and Asana, allowing teams to use the tools and processes they are already comfortable with and giving admins, developers, and architects a way to collaborate on Salesforce projects effectively.

2 **Gearset has the industry's deepest understanding of Salesforce DevOps, with over two thousand paid deployments.** The rep would mention that Gearset has more than four times the number of Salesforce DevOps deployments as the nearest competitor, including some of the world's biggest brands, like IBM and Johnson & Johnson. They are the most trusted partner for Salesforce DevOps. They would also make the point that everyone on the team, from the founders to the folks in support and sales, has a deep understanding of the problems Salesforce teams face and are here to help ensure customer success.

3 **Gearset has both broad and deep capabilities focused on the most important problems for Salesforce DevOps teams.** The rep would show a demo of some of Gearset's advanced functionality to speed up Salesforce releases, including comparisons and precision deployments for end users, and release pipelines for leads and architects. The rep would also mention (and potentially demo) the breadth of Gearset's offering, with backup functionality and support for Revenue Cloud.

April says: The pitch winds up with a case study example of a specific customer, and ends with a discussion about how to get started using Gearset.

TRANSLATING THE STORYBOARD INTO A SALES PITCH

· ·

Congratulations! You have a storyboard for your sales pitch. Next, you need to turn the storyboard into a pitch your reps can use.

Where and How to Use Slides, a Demo, and a Script

Building the final sales pitch generally involves a team effort between marketing and sales. Marketing can help with crafting slides, getting graphics created, and wordsmithing the script. Sales needs to ensure that what gets built fits the timeline of a first conversation and makes sense in the context of a sales call.

Do You Really Need a Standard Deck and a Script?

Every mature sales organization I know has a standard first-call sales pitch deck that reps are trained to use and that comes with some form of script that teaches them what to say. Some start-ups I've worked with are uncomfortable with the idea of

"Don't sell
life insurance.
Sell what life
insurance can do."

BEN FELDMAN

a "scripted" deck because they worry that the sales reps will simply repeat the script like robots. Obviously, you don't want sales robots, but you do want to get some standardization in the first call for several reasons.

First and foremost, a standardized first-call deck ensures that you are consistently positioning your offerings in the best way you can. You agreed on your positioning at the executive team level, using everything you know about your customers, competitors, and differentiated value. You need to ensure that you are telling your best story to every prospect.

Second, a standardized deck makes it much easier to onboard new reps. Your most experienced salespeople might know enough to wing their way through a pitch, but a new rep never will. As you scale, fast onboarding becomes critically important.

Third, it's impossible to measure and learn what's working and what isn't if every rep is having a different conversation in the first call. Standardization helps you understand when and where things need to change.

The script can take the form of a word-by-word story or simply be a series of bullet points and suggestions. Either works fine, in my opinion, and you should expect sales reps, as they get comfortable with the story, to improvise and add their own flair to it. What you don't want to see are reps significantly changing the story to the point at which you have lost the flow completely, or you are no longer centered on your differentiated value.

There is also a tendency for sales reps to drift off message over time. The mature sales organizations I have worked with will periodically "recertify" reps on the pitch by having them pitch to the sales executive to ensure that the story remains consistent. Without regular check-ins, it becomes very hard to ensure that your sales team is delivering the message in a consistent way over time.

Slides versus a Conversation

Different companies will choose different ways to communicate each step of the pitch. Some teams prefer to use slides; others will choose to simply have a conversation. Some products show well in a demo and others don't. Some companies like to have a full, detailed script, and others stick with bullet points. Regardless of how you choose to build out the pitch, you will need to make it consumable to your sales reps.

Step 1, Insight: The Insight step is generally done with a slide (or multiple slides). I find it helps in making your point very clear to the prospect. I've also seen reps very effectively do the entire setup phase in a quick conversation with the customer.

Step 2, Alternatives: The competitive pros and cons can be done in a wide variety of ways. I've always used a very simple table for this step, but I'm careful to keep the number of words to a minimum. I like having a visual reference, but I don't want the prospect reading a slide when we should be having a discovery conversation. In my experience, the script for this slide works best if you give reps the key pros and cons of each solution in bullet form, plus a set of questions they can work into a discovery conversation. We generally expect this step to be free-flowing, so I would not expect reps to stick to a strict script here, but I would expect them to find a way to make their key points and ask the key questions. The route reps take to get there can vary.

Step 3, The Perfect World: This step can be done easily with or without a slide. Sometimes I like to position this as the conclusion to our discovery conversation and leave it at that. If The Perfect World has several points, sometimes I like to have a slide just to reiterate those points.

Step 4, The Introduction: The Introduction is generally done with a slide. Often, it will include a graphic to help introduce the offering, particularly when the offering is a suite or platform, or if you are introducing everything the company delivers.

Step 5, Differentiated Value: Differentiated Value is often done with a demo, but it doesn't need to be. For highly customizable products, I've seen companies do this step with slides, or slides with screenshots, and then use a customized demo later in the sales process. If you do intend to use a demo, the demo flow needs to follow the value themes. I often use a slide to introduce the value themes, then run the demo, and then wrap up with a slide that reiterates the value themes again at the end. You should script this demo, but how much scripting you use is totally up to you. I prefer to have a full, detailed script that a brand-new rep can use without assistance from a sales engineer. As a rep gets more comfortable with the demo, they can then improvise, as long as they are sticking to the value themes.

Step 6, Proof: The Proof step is often a case study, a logo slide, and potentially some "sparklers," like awards or accolades, and is usually done with slides.

Step 7, Objections: How you present the optional Objections step will depend on the message you need to communicate. It is done either with a slide or a scripted talk track for the rep.

Step 8, The Ask: The Ask can be a slide or scripted discussion.

NOW YOU have a set of slides, a demo, and a script your sales team can use for a first call with a prospect. But we aren't quite at the finish line yet. Next, we need to validate that the pitch works and then roll it out to the sales team. We also want to start thinking about how the sales narrative will be used beyond sales calls.

PART
FIVE

TESTING AND LAUNCHING THE SALES PITCH

· ·

Once you have a deck, demo, and script, you are ready to test the pitch. Here are a few things to think about as you move into the validation phase.

Testing the Pitch

Once a group has developed a new sales pitch, the team is often excited and wants to roll it out as quickly as possible. I think it makes more sense to make sure you have it validated in a more controlled way by doing a limited test before you roll it out to the entire sales team.

Getting the sales team to adopt a new sales pitch is often much harder than you think it is going to be. Your reps have spent weeks, months, maybe years, working with the current pitch and, even if they have complaints about the way the product is positioned or the flow of the demo, they are comfortable with what they are doing today. It is going to take some effort for them to get to that same level of comfort with anything new. New stuff is hard to pitch, and at the start, those pitches are going to be stilted and somewhat awkward until people are more familiar with the material. It is completely normal for reps to dislike a new sales pitch, even when it is clearly better than the old one.

My recommendation is to start with one salesperson, preferably someone the rest of the team looks up to and respects. Ideally, that rep was involved at least partially in creating the deck, demo, and script, so they are already familiar with the content. Marketing and sales leaders should make sure this rep is trained and comfortable with the flow and timing of the pitch. Once the rep is ready, they can start testing the pitch with real, qualified prospects.

Test, Discuss, Iterate (within Limits)

Ideally, during the testing phase, the folks who created the sales pitch should be listening to each call the rep is doing. After every call, the team should sit down and compare notes on what they felt did and did not work in the meeting.

- Where was the prospect getting lost?

- Where was the prospect getting excited?

- Were there questions asked that might indicate there was something confusing in the pitch?

There may be obvious adjustments you want to make. These are usually related to specific wording or vocabulary that customers find confusing. Sometimes, a prospect will bring up an objection that can be handled easily with a small adjustment to the pitch. Other times, you will notice that you are missing something in the setup related to a specific alternative approach that needs to be addressed more directly. Be careful, however, that you don't start to iterate on anything that is a core part of the sales pitch itself. It's fine to make smaller changes, but you don't want to ruin the test by substantially changing the pitch itself.

The Pass/Fail Criteria

Most metrics we use to measure the effectiveness of a sales pitch take a long time to measure. In the short term, it's often hard to measure empirically whether or not the pitch is working. In the long term, upgrading your sales pitch will drive an improvement across a range of sales metrics. For example, you would expect to see more leads progressing to the next phase of your sales process, as well as bad leads dropping out early in your process, and an upswing in close rates down the line as a result. As the marketing team starts to adopt the story, your overall lead quality should improve, along with a corresponding improvement in sales metrics. However, if your sales cycles are long—weeks and months as opposed to days—or you have a very high average deal size and therefore a low volume of pitches to test on, you might need to move forward with less hard evidence and more qualitative indicators that the pitch is or is not working.

My advice on this is to rely on the expertise and experience of the salesperson with whom you have selected to run the pitch testing. Once that sales rep is reasonably comfortable with the storyline and has done a few pitches, you can start looking for feedback from them. I would call a new pitch validated when these two criteria are met:

1 **The rep feels the pitch no longer needs further refinement or iterations.** Although the rep may still want more experience to tune the finer details, they are satisfied with the overall flow of the pitch.

We don't know if
we have the best
story possible, but
we know if it's better
than the old one.

2   **The rep has made a decision to use the new pitch because it is clearly better than the old one.** This is the key. If your best salesperson thinks this sales pitch works better than the old pitch, despite their obvious bias toward a pitch that they are already experienced and comfortable with, take that as a sign that you should move forward and roll the pitch out to the rest of the team. Conversely, if your best salesperson has used the pitch several times, is no longer interested in iterating on it, and still feels the old pitch is better, you should consider that a failed test and head back to the drawing board.

What Happens if the Test Fails?

In my experience working with companies on sales pitches, a failed test at this stage is rare, but it can happen. If the best minds, with the most customer knowledge in the company, are involved in creating the pitch, it would be surprising if they came up with something that didn't work. If the pitch fails, there are usually two root causes: either the sales team wasn't involved enough in the creation of the pitch, or the pitch doesn't work because the positioning is weak.

Fixing the first of those root causes is a matter of running the sales pitch creation process again, with more involvement from salespeople who have experience with customers in the early stages of deals. If the sales team is already heavily involved in creating the pitch, then the culprit is weak inputs to the pitch creation process. And if that is the case, the team will need to go back and formally review their positioning. My previous book, *Obviously Awesome*, outlines a process for getting to the best positioning for your product—obviously, I would suggest you start there.

Rolling the New Pitch Out to the Sales Team

Once the pitch has been validated by one rep, they can help you roll it out to the rest of the team. For the training package, I suggest making a video of that rep doing a pitch, plus a Q&A. You will need to give reps a way to get some experience with the new pitch by doing practice pitches, and generally you want to make sure they are tested on the new pitch with someone from the sales leadership team before they start pitching to prospects. It also helps to include the sales rep who was involved in the test phase. That rep will have more credibility with the sales team than your marketers will, and they are better equipped to answer more specific sales-related questions.

Who Owns the Sales Pitch?

I often get asked who should "own" the sales pitch after it is developed. I believe in cross-functional teams to create positioning and the sales pitch, but I do think it makes sense to designate someone to be responsible for stewardship of positioning and the sales pitch. Because positioning and the sales pitch are closely tied, ideally we have someone who is responsible for both.

If a product marketing function exists in your company, this is the natural place for the positioning and sales narrative to land. That person will be responsible for documenting both positioning and the sales pitches, as well as any approved assets that go with it, such as graphics or illustrations. They will also be responsible for ensuring that there are regular check-in meetings with the cross-functional team to review the positioning to determine if a shift is needed. If the team decides that a shift in positioning is needed, the sales pitch will also need to be adjusted to reflect that shift.

Common Mistakes
. . . .

I started using a version of this pitch structure fifteen years ago, first when I was an in-house marketing executive, and then later as a consultant. Over that time, I've built over two hundred pitches with companies, and I've seen what works, what doesn't, and where teams get stuck. Here are some common mistakes and things to watch out for.

Insight That Isn't Unique
Some companies will try to use a common industry trend as insight at the start of their sales pitch, rather than the company's unique insight into the market. For example, I have seen variations of "Companies are generating more data than ever before," or "The pace of AI adoption is accelerating," or "Companies need to digitally transform their businesses." All of these are obvious trends in the market. The key to Step 1, Insight, is to go beyond these surface-level observations and get down to the insight that makes your solution uniquely valuable. Your insight should be unique and differentiated because you need it to set up the reasoning behind why your unique, differentiated value is important.

A Lack of Discovery
Experienced sales reps will naturally see Step 2, Alternatives, as a place to do discovery. Less-experienced reps may fall into a trap of talking *at* a prospect, rather than taking the

time to ask questions to make sure their characterization of the market is resonating with the prospect and that they are getting what they need to fully understand the prospect's situation. That doesn't necessarily mean you need to spend a long time on this step—it will depend on how many alternative approaches you want to cover and the complexity of their pros and cons. The key in this step is to make sure the prospect sees their current situation and choices in the picture you paint of the market before you move on.

Spending Too Much Time on the Setup Phase

One of the most common mistakes companies make with this format is spending too much time on the setup phase. The first call with a prospect can last anywhere from thirty minutes to an hour. Most companies can get through the setup part of the pitch in a few minutes, depending on how active the discussion with the prospect is. I've seen companies do the setup in as little as ninety seconds, but others that need up to ten minutes.

The setup is important, and you should never skip it. But you need to spend the bulk of your time ensuring that the prospect grasps your differentiated value. The setup provides important context so your prospect understands the importance of that value, but don't forget that your value is the meat of that first call.

Weak or Undifferentiated Value Themes

Your positioning is the fundamental input to the sales pitch. Weak positioning leads to a weak insight statement and will result in an ineffective story about how you are differentiated from the alternatives. Your Differentiated Value step is the most important input to the pitch because this is where

"The customer's perception is your reality."

KATE ZABRISKIE

you articulate what your solution can do for prospects that no alternative solution can deliver. If that value is weak or not very differentiated, then the pitch will not be compelling and is unlikely to work.

Proof That Doesn't Match the Prospect's Situation

In Step 6, Proof, some companies default to sharing a case study, and often use the same case study for every prospect. If your prospects are similar, this might be fine. But ideally you want your proof to connect to both the value themes you've covered and the individual prospect's situation. Wherever possible, you want to have proof that matches the prospect. For example, if you are using a case study, it should reflect a similar industry or show a similar use case, such as moving from the same status quo solution.

An Ask That's Too Complicated

Buyers don't necessarily know how to evaluate and purchase solutions. So, it's your job to make sure that the ask is straightforward and doesn't cause the prospect to second-guess whether they should accept your recommendation for how to move ahead. The Ask step should move the deal forward (assuming the prospect is a good fit for your solution) by giving the prospect a next step that is easy to say yes to.

Rolling Out the Sales Pitch and Then Forgetting about It

Even if you manage to build, test, and roll out your pitch, the work isn't done. As I mentioned earlier, someone needs to assume ownership of the sales pitch, and there should be checks in place to ensure that:

- **New reps are trained to do the pitch properly.** Ideally, training materials are developed and there is some test or certification to ensure that any new rep can do the pitch correctly before they start pitching to prospects.

- **The pitch isn't warping over time.** In general, pitches tend to change over time as reps start to make often unintended small changes. The best way to ensure this doesn't happen is to have regular check-ins or scheduled pitch recertifications.

- **The pitch gets updated as needed.** The sales pitch is a reflection of your company positioning, which will change when there are major shifts in your offerings or competitive landscape. When those changes happen, the pitch needs to shift to reflect the new positioning.

USING YOUR SALES PITCH STORY BEYOND SALES CALLS

This book is about how to build a sales pitch, so naturally we have focused on how the pitch gets used in a sales call. But that isn't the only place this story will be used.

In particular, once the pitch is developed, it will become a key input to your company's marketing messaging and can be used either directly or indirectly in different types of marketing content. A sales pitch that is built through this methodology uses your positioning as a foundation. Therefore, it has the same core differentiated value, which you determine as part of your positioning, at the core of your marketing messaging. Building a sales pitch in this manner ensures that the story you are telling in marketing is aligned with the story you are telling in sales.

Most company home pages start with a tagline and then communicate their differentiated value themes. A company home page typically doesn't follow a story structure per se—and it doesn't need to. However, there are a million and one ways the positioning story can and should be incorporated into the company's marketing. Let's look at a few examples.

The Explainer Video

Many companies have a short video on their home page that tells the story of who they are and the value they deliver. Using the sales pitch structure for that video ensures you are clearly communicating your unique insight on the market, how you are different from competitors, the value only you can deliver, and the proof you can do what you say you can. You can choose how much or how little detail you want to get into, but you have time to work through most, if not all, steps of the pitch, even in a couple of minutes.

The Buyer's Guide

One of my favorite categories of marketing content is the buyer's guide. As I told you at the beginning of this book, many prospects have never purchased a product like yours before. They are desperate for information that can help them make choices they feel comfortable with and can also defend to their boss and other stakeholders. A buyer's guide is a great way to walk prospects though what you believe a knowledgeable buyer should consider. It is also a great piece of lead generation content—a prospect's interest in a buyer's guide is a strong signal that they are currently shopping for software in your space.

I've created dozens of buyer's guides, and each one has included pieces that came from my sales pitch. A good guide gives buyers a way to think about purchase criteria. It may include checklists of features that a buyer should look for, but more importantly, it helps buyers understand when and why they should be looking for those features. The insight from your sales pitch (Step 1) is often a good starting point for a buyer's guide because it helps customers understand what's important. The buyer's guide can educate customers on how certain important features map to value and give them a way to determine whether that value is important to their business. Using the Alternatives step in the sales pitch, you can then build categorized value/feature checklists with commentary suggesting which customers should include what features in their purchase criteria.

Telling the Story Using the Product Itself, Including Onboarding, Tutorials, and Help

Many companies with sales teams have a free version of their product or a free trial that is essentially the start of their sales process. In these "product-led" sales motions, the product itself and the experience a prospect has with the product are where many expectations for the offering are set.

Developing a clear story around your differentiated value is a very good place to start when thinking about how you want a customer to learn about and experience the product. That story, or components of it, can be represented in onboarding materials, assisted walkthroughs, tips, help materials, and more. Your differentiated value and how your product delivers it should be made obvious to prospects as they make their way through initial product onboarding and during their first experiences with the product.

One caution here, however. It is not uncommon for a company to have a version of the product that end users can freely download and use, and for the sales team to later sell an enterprise contract to a different, management-level buyer. In these cases, often the end-user positioning is different from the positioning for the economic champion, and therefore the sales pitch for the ultimate buyer will be different from the narrative for end users. The important point here is that if you are telling a story through the product itself, it is essential to understand what story you are telling and to whom.

Visual Elements

Most companies could and should take advantage of representing their company or product using a well-thought-out graphic. There are a few different graphics you can use to communicate your differentiation and position in the market. Here are a few examples:

- The product suite

- The company portfolio

- The "how we fit into your current infrastructure" illustration

- The workflow graphic, which shows how a particular use case or workflow gets done. The goal is to highlight a specific value point, such as "saves time" or "eliminates manual processes."

A visual can do a lot to position your offering and tell a story about how you are different from your competitors. You can find some examples in the downloadable materials available at **aprildunford.com/books**.

"A well-told story is a gift to the reader/ listener/viewer because it teaches them how to confront their own discomforts."

SHAWN COYNE

The Conference Talk

I've worked with a number of founders who regularly speak at conferences. While I don't believe it is appropriate to do a sales pitch as a conference talk, there are components of the pitch that are perfectly suited to a conference talk. The setup phase of the sales pitch is centered on your insight into the market. That insight is often a great topic for a conference talk. It gives the speaker a chance to expose their thinking about the market while providing valuable information and insights to the audience. Pay attention to the start-up CEOs you see speaking at conferences—many of them are speaking about what they have learned about the space they are in and how they formed a unique point of view on the market.

Research, White Papers, and Other Content

Similar to the conference talk, some companies will sponsor or conduct research that explores the themes of their market insight, and then distribute the results of that research in a white paper or other marketing content. Many companies will publish yearly research that tracks trends and the adoption of solutions in the market. All of this should be aligned with and could even feed into the Insight step of your sales pitch. Results and conclusions from this type of research are often easily repurposed into blog posts, social media content, and other materials.

A Book

· · · · · · · · ·

Companies can make good use of books to communicate their insight in particular. The co-founders of HubSpot, Brian Halligan and Dharmesh Shah, famously wrote *Inbound Marketing* to articulate how marketing was changing and how companies should be reacting to that change. You may have noticed already, but the book you are reading right now follows this same sales pitch structure. Hey, it would be a little strange if I didn't use my own sales pitch structure to sell you on, well, my sales pitch structure. It's so meta.

THESE ARE just some examples to get your creative juices flowing. One of the most creative examples I have seen is Postman's graphic novel, *The API-First World*. There are no limits to the creative ways your marketing team can communicate your sales story using content.

CONCLUSION

· · · · · · · · · · · · · · · ·

SELLING IS INCREDIBLY HARD. Good salespeople will spend years developing their skills, and some of them will never master them. However, building a good sales pitch doesn't need to be difficult. If you stay focused on helping the buyer make a confident decision, you will end up with a pitch that works. Here are a few key takeaways I'd like to leave you with:

1 **Buying is hard.** Do not underestimate how difficult making a purchase decision can be for your prospects.

2 **"Do nothing" is the most fearsome competitor you have.** If customers cannot figure out how to confidently make a purchase decision, they simply won't make one.

3 **A sales pitch is special.** Companies tell different stories for different audiences and for different purposes. A sales pitch is a unique style of story designed to guide the customer to a place where they can say yes with confidence.

4 **A great sales pitch starts with your company's unique insight into the market.** Sales pitches that start with generic problems or trends will not lead prospects to your unique differentiated value.

5 **Help customers understand their options and they will be better informed to make decisions confidently.** You don't need to bash the competition to do this.

6 **Differentiated value is the star of the show.** Customers don't care about features. They care about what those features can do for their business.

Knowing how to do something is not the same thing as teaching someone else how to do it. This is my attempt to teach something I've been doing for decades and is one of the most nuanced skills I've developed in my career. I hope you found a shortcut here to something useful and valuable for your business.

Stay focused on helping the buyer make a confident decision.

PHOTO: DAVID CHANG

ABOUT THE AUTHOR

APRIL DUNFORD is the world's leading expert on product positioning. She has worked with hundreds of fast-growing technology companies to accelerate their growth through clear, compelling positioning. Previously, she ran marketing and product teams at a series of successful technology start-ups. April is also a board member, investor, and advisor to dozens of high-growth businesses, and is the author of the bestselling book *Obviously Awesome: How to Nail Product Positioning so Customers Get It, Buy It, Love It.*

HOW TO
LEARN MORE

. . . .

If you have made it this far and are interested in going beyond what's in this book, I have some resources for you.

Templates

As mentioned throughout the book, you can download the latest version of the sales pitch templates from my website at **aprildunford.com/books**.

Podcast and Articles

I have my own podcast, *Positioning with April Dunford*, where I do a deeper exploration of many of the concepts covered in both of my books. I also have occasional guests including CEOs I have worked with, and experts whose work is related to positioning and building a great sales pitch. I frequently highlight those conversations on my website, or you can search for "April Dunford" and "podcast" to get a more complete list of those conversations.

I also write regularly about positioning and sales pitches. You can follow me on LinkedIn at **linkedin.com/in/aprildunford** or subscribe to my email list at **aprildunford.com/books**.

Consulting

For individual technology companies that want help from me directly, I run a facilitated workshop. During our sessions, I work with you and your executive team, facilitating the group through the component pieces of your positioning and then creating a sales narrative that maps to it. You can find out more about my current consulting offerings at **aprildunford.com**.

Printed in Great Britain
by Amazon

32770989R00138